T0330859

Organizational Aesthetics

Organizational Aesthetics attempts to reconstruct artful representations of the organizational world and businesspeople. It looks at organizations and management through the eyes of artists, painters, and photographers and decodes meanings contained in artistic messages, grasping the aesthetic perceptions of the world of management and organization. Paintings and photos are analysed using qualitative methods from the social sciences as well as from the art analysis tradition. The novelty of the presented approach rests in the original method of parallel dialogues, taking place both in the institutional sphere and between co-authors. The institutional aspect covers a practical, business perspective and extends the narrow framework of a single discipline. It complements academic rigour with elements of digression and free conversation, revealing a variety of nuances for which conventional research paradigms do not always allow. Readers will receive a proposal on how to integrate different approaches to organizational analysis stemming from artistic, managerial, and academic experiences.

Barbara Fryzel, PhD, dr habil. is an economist and an associate professor at Jagiellonian University in Krakow. She has multiple years of managerial experience in international corporations. She is a laureate of the Foundation for Polish Science and was a visiting post-doc scholar at University College London. Her interests include organizational culture, corporate social responsibility, and behavioural ethics.

Aleksander Marcinkowski, Ph.D., is Senior Lecturer at the Jagiellonian University. His research interests include sociology of organization, organizational culture, and entrepreneurship. He has participated in international research projects on attitudes towards entrepreneurship (in cooperation with Michigan University), on the role of traditional industrial branches in the contemporary European economy (V Framework Program of EU) and on Institutional Development Programs in state and self-government administration (multilateral research done in cooperation with University of Economics, Kraków, Canadian Urban Institute and Polish Ministry of Home Affairs). He was a visiting scholar at the Johns Hopkins University – Bologna Center.

Routledge Focus on Business and Management

The fields of business and management have grown exponentially as areas of research and education. This growth presents challenges for readers trying to keep up with the latest important insights. *Routledge Focus on Business and Management* presents small books on big topics and how they intersect with the world of business research.

Individually, each title in the series provides coverage of a key academic topic, whilst collectively, the series forms a comprehensive collection across the business disciplines.

Healthy Ageing after COVID-19
Research and Policy Perspectives from Asia
Edited by Wang-Kin Chiu and Vincent T.S. Law

Entrepreneurial Attributes
Accessing Your Inner Entrepreneur For Business and Beyond
Andrew Clarke

Leadership and Strategic Management
Decision-Making in Times of Change
Paolo Boccardelli and Federica Brunetta

Artificial Intelligence and Project Management
An Integrated Approach to Knowledge-Based Evaluation
Tadeusz A. Grzeszczyk

Organizational Aesthetics
Artful Visual Representations of Business and Organizations
Barbara Fryzel and Aleksander Marcinkowski

For more information about this series, please visit: www.routledge.com/ Routledge-Focus-on-Business-and-Management/book-series/FBM

Organizational Aesthetics
Artful Visual Representations of
Business and Organizations

Barbara Fryzel
and
Aleksander Marcinkowski

Routledge
Taylor & Francis Group

NEW YORK AND LONDON

First published 2024
by Routledge
605 Third Avenue, New York, NY 10158

and by Routledge
4 Park Square, Milton Park, Abingdon, Oxon, OX14 4RN

Routledge is an imprint of the Taylor & Francis Group, an informa business

ISBN: 978-1-032-79235-4 (hbk)
ISBN: 978-1-032-80500-9 (pbk)
ISBN: 978-1-003-49710-3 (ebk)

DOI: 10.4324/9781003497103

Typeset in Times New Roman
by Apex CoVantage, LLC

Contents

Introduction
Watching from the riverbank

The inspiration to write this book came from our interest in the evolution of social perception of management as a scientific discipline and attitudes towards people of organizations. Organizations could only become an object of a more generalized perception after they had arisen as key social institutions, existing in social awareness along with their personnel, in the role of architects of revolution, social change, or progress, efficient organizers of other people's working conditions, a source of oppression, power, and control, and sometimes of harm and wrong in society, or ugliness and roughness of things – effects of mass production, standardization, and relentless pursuit of maximum profit.

Initially, management as an emerging field of study did not attract popular attention, and processes taking place in workshops and factories, usually associated with towns increasingly influencing social life, were not publicly debated in the 16th or 17th century. However, in time, as observers of social relations became increasingly aware of, and sensitive to, the penetration by organizations of all aspects of human life, the perception of the important role of organizations in social structures has become clearer. Undoubtedly, that perception and the related visual experience are influenced by the omnipresence of the picture used to convey not so much a factual message as associated emotions and its authors' interpretation. Pictures in mass media, films, newspapers, or in more sophisticated paintings and photographs form the set of daily representations of the world around us, in which a major role is played not only by people but also by institutions and organizations.

Organizations have become part of daily experience, and the way they are experienced depends on the type of sensitivity which is defined in the research paradigm adopted by researchers.

The *experience* of management as a social phenomenon was not possible until the effects of its practices became *embodied* in social structures, patterns, norms, and values. Only then did these effects begin to be perceived by society, to encourage reflection, inspire researchers, writers, painters, and photographers, as well as philosophers and ideologues who propagated the mission of people of organizations in the new industrial world (Burnham,

DOI: 10.4324/9781003497103-1

1941). This social awareness of management did not emerge at once. It was built gradually but continually over the 19th century. In 1835, Charles Babbage published a treaty in which he advocated for a scientific approach to organization and management, emphasizing the importance of planning and division of work (Babbage, 1835). It was three decades after Eli Whitney demonstrated in 1801 the method of mass production, showing how to assemble firearms from piles of replaceable parts (completing an order for 15,000 firearms for the newly formed American army, see www.americanheritage.com/eli-whitneys-other-talent?page=show, accessed 1.11.2023). Ideas and knowledge of inventors, entrepreneurs, and, slightly later, scientists were with increasing frequency materialized and *embodied* in new methods of organization, new products, and new services. The world saturated with technology and techniques produced further innovative solutions, some with a groundbreaking character, deeply changing culture and the social structure. An example is given by the origins of a massive cultural configuration built around its central object, a car popularized by Henry Ford. It soon became evident that the use of this *embodied* idea of freedom and free movement was conditional on developing infrastructure which created new markets, new services, and new social behaviours. Paved roads were necessary with related facilities: filling stations, motels, catering establishments. The need arose for road traffic regulations, driving schools and licences, car repair shops, courses of study educating engineers for the purposes of the automotive industry, and designers-stylists. Finally, recognition of the car as an element of American culture gave rise to a special film genre known as 'road movies' with its cult productions, such as Easy Rider (1969), Rain Man (1988), or Thelma and Louise (1991). This example illustrates convincingly how organization and management can become an area of more popular interest and part of the experience of large populations.

Ideas become *embodied*, and similarly *experience* of the environment and of consequences of the organization and management processes can have an *embodied* aspect, when sensory perception of the environment, visual, auditory, tactile, or perception of spaces in which we stay builds experience with an aesthetic nature, releasing emotions.

For example, there is one type of experience of the bank, as an institution embodying the need for ensured safety of buying and selling transactions and for stable deposit rates, in the case of someone who wishes to build up savings, and another type of experience in the case of a player who is ready to take risk and seeks suitable financial instruments. In the former case, an important role is performed by the architectural aesthetic that conveys a clear message of stability and power of that institution through its frequent references to classical beauty of Greek or Roman temples.[1] The aesthetic associated with the architecture of banks represents the embodiment of their founders' dreams of true strength, and perhaps even of banks' 'perpetuity' as key institutions organizing social and economic life. Customers who wish to make deposits or obtain access to loans and seek assurance and stability can experience the guarantee of peace of mind at a bank where the idea of the world of finance is embodied in architecture that dominates the environment.

Another picture emerges in the latter case. Indeed, there is also space for gamblers who seek a thrill of excitement in betting on venture investments that may end in a heavy loss or considerable profit. The bank then becomes a casino space where the pool of funds is subject to a sophisticated game, and the accompanying emotions are quite different from those felt by deposit holders who want to build up savings. The experience is thus determined by a number of factors, and although it takes place in a theoretically formally defined space, it may be highly idiosyncratic. Researchers have the privilege of observing that experience and their perception depend on various types of sensitivity embodied in a specific perspective or research method adopted. From up close, details can be perceived – either the artist's brush strokes and the texture of painting or micro-phenomena – variables at the level of individuals in an organization. From the distance, we have a better view of the entire structure of the observed reality – either the composition and play of colours and light in a painting or macro-phenomena – situational variables defining a market or an industry.

The experience of banks is thus different in the case of someone who makes deposits than in the case of an investor who is willing to take risk and has just won a bet with the market, after placing a wager on chosen mutual funds offered by the bank. There is one picture of the organization viewed from the perspective of a saver who makes deposits and another from the perspective of an investor and a player. Similarly, one picture of reality is obtained by a participant observer (an insider looking from within the organization), taking part in the life of the organization, and another by a researcher, an observer watching it from up close, from the distance, directly or in some reflection. Metaphorically, the situation can be compared to us sitting relaxed in the afternoon on a riverbank, from which we are watching the landscape on the other side, or the world reflected in water, that is represented by an intervening medium, (as used, e.g., in painting, message-carrying layer, pastel, tempera, oil, etc.), as if we looked in a mirror through which our interpretation is mediated.

Research or methodological decisions made lead to various pictures of the organization. Even an observer who prefers a perspective from the distance, while sitting on the riverbank, may look at his watch to find an external, temporal point of reference for his observations or may omit exact measurement to focus instead on the visual experience as such, watching tall buildings of the financial district in the distance that will also create a specific picture in his mind.

Organizational aesthetics as a method of research on embodied experience is close to the examination of the picture of the world reflected on the surface of the water observed from the riverbank that offers a specific view – sometimes lit, sometimes covered by a veil of mystery.

Directing attention to those themes and aspects greatly inspires methodology and the observation that the development of organizations, improvement of management methods, and reflection on the state of academic knowledge of management and organization can be significantly enhanced by drawing inspiration that comes from aesthetics, also by turning to unorthodox methods, open to other disciplines, of conceptualizing reality, recording events and emotions which accompany phenomena that are considered to be characteristic, unusual, surprising. Dilemmas and multiple methodological choices are well illustrated by polysemy characteristic of the word 'bank', which facilitates a metaphoric illustration of the research approach we adopted.

In the book we give the Reader, we wish to examine what perception of the world of organizations and business is transmitted using the visual arts of painting and photography, and how aesthetic principles of a specific style correspond to change in the perception of business and businesspeople

By proposing a method designed to reveal the aesthetic experience of the organization and the inspiring role of that experience for cognition and research, we aim at finding, following the example of painters, better light that will disclose the depth and nuances of the world of organizations, while we fully accept that this perspective is far from a cool, positivist examination of reality, and we may not expect that it will produce statistically representative results.

We seek new inspirations, also methodological, that can be used to see the topics of our interest in another new light, in new categories and classes of datasets that can be found in works created by artists: painters, writers, filmmakers, photographers. Their visions reveal various aspects of management, organizations, various personality traits of people of importance in that world, and the consequences of their activity. A starting point for those visions is the social 'visibility' of management. We aim to examine how various understandings of management appeared in aesthetic categories, what aesthetic means of expression, and what symbols were associated with discovering the nature of management, its subject, and its object by the artists who portrayed or took photographs of figures, situations, and circumstances related to specific social roles being performed in the world of organizations. In our opinion, the aesthetic vision of the reality of management, emerging from paintings and photographs, may be used to obtain inspiring data that brings new knowledge; those aesthetic records and depictions of organizations form a bank of knowledge and aesthetic evidence. This strand of thought is guided by a reflection once formulated by Rollo May (1994, p. 31 ff). He observed that artists are distinguished by a special type of creativity that enables them to experience the future condition of society, tensions, conflicts and crises, collective effervescence, and sometimes.

One question has to be explained, namely that of work openness as understood by Umberto Eco. He wrote:

> if I was to synthetically define the subject matter of the present enquiry, I would refer to a certain concept, unanimously accepted today by many

aesthetic theories: an artwork as a message is essentially indefinite, is carrying multiple meanings that co-exist in a single signifier

(Eco, 1994, p. 4)

Importantly, Eco applied his theory principally to artworks – he considered them to be highly ambiguous and invited audiences to more actively participate in the process of work creation and interpretation. It should be mentioned that the theory of open work met with lively criticism (Mallac, 1971). However, that criticism did not undermine the importance of Eco as a pioneer who encouraged discussion among researchers.

We imagine that while meeting with the described works, every spectator will experience (in the literal meaning of the word, since organizational aesthetics is a perspective based on sensory experience of reality) those works in an individual way, and the visual experience will result in personal interpretations. In other words, each of us has an individual perception. Individual interpretative thoughts that the Reader can add, for own purposes, to our conclusions and observations will constitute a continuation of the narrative we constructed, in which everyone can personally take on the role of co-designer, according to the principle of an open work with an ending that is adaptable and co-authored by its reader or spectator.

We could not reproduce in this book all works included in our research; however, most of them are available online. We encourage the Reader to join us in this reflection by individual contemplation of those works. Their detailed list is contained in an Appendix 1.

Material culture evolves. Surely, new works will appear, especially in modern painting or photography, addressing more or less directly the topic of organizations and business. Thus, the open character of the organizational tale we propose will realize not only in the activity of our readers and spectators of the works but also in the activity of artists whose perception of our environment may reveal many new and surprising ways of looking at the reality of organizations.

Note

1. We refer here to emblematic examples of great commercial architecture, such as the Gibson Hall building, the historical headquarters of a bank, or the more recently erected Ciudad Santander, described in more detail in the chapter titled 'Architecture of metaphors and associations', and not to the rather uninspiring local branches of today's banks with their controversial and quite accidental aesthetic that can be the subject matter of a separate study.

1 Knowledge hidden in sight

1.1 Fluctuating paradigms

We happen to be tired of, or even discouraged by, traditionally sanctioned, ritualized methods of doing research. Many of us follow the positivist approach and still tend to see the model for all disciplines in the methodological achievements of the natural sciences. There are also a great number of those who departed from that model, principally attracted by the propositions put forward by postmodernism that promised liberated imagination and unrestricted creativity instead of submitting to the full rigour of the method; however, the postmodernist perspective has turned into a tradition like previously positivism. Thus, we have two traditions: positivism and postmodernism with their correlates – realism and subjectivism in the field of ontology; seeking generalizations and descriptions of unique phenomena; and neutral records of facts and data interpretation. This 'battle of paradigms' has to be recalled to realize a distinct change in the background of reflection on the state of science in general and of the social sciences and their methodology in particular. Today, proposals aimed at changing the methodological model of research are put forward not in opposition to the patterns of scientific thought known from the past but with reference to the social context of science and the consequences of its situation in that context. A response to this new situation in science and to new functions of scientific knowledge may be given by the proposed new mode of developing the scientific method, known as Mode 2 (Novotny et al., 2003).

In the field of management studies, that change has undoubtedly been triggered by a new phenomenon: organizations have 'blurred'. Their boundaries are different from those perceived some 50 years ago. Constituent components of an organization are not easy to identify. Today, we consider the relational existence of enterprises, corporations, or other social entities.

Another notable change has taken place in the understanding of knowledge in management. The emergence of such concepts as a knowledge society, knowledge economy, or knowledge management in a narrower understanding required that attention be focused on the very concept of knowledge and

DOI: 10.4324/9781003497103-2

on perceiving its evolution. The knowledge of management has expanded to topics previously excluded from its scope. Emotionality has become a dimension of governance and managerial decisions, a parameter of corporate life. Knowledge is no longer monopolized by universities.[1] Knowledge may be generated by companies, other organizations, even individuals who gain a special type of experience (Nonaka & Takeuchi, 2000).[2] Research problems are being defined today in a complex interactive context, for example in large EU framework programmes. The growing influence of institutions financing research may cause some concern. Today, these institutions are capable of defining the main directions of research in many scientific disciplines.

We address these topics in the following sections of this study to confront them with our research purpose, namely exploring those cognitive images of management or its cognitive representations (models, propositions, assumptions) which emerge from a research process oriented to dialogue, negotiation, consultation and interactions between researchers that precede traditionally understood definitions of goals, of a problem, a heuristic model, research topics, and (possibly) hypotheses, and lead to adopting criteria for the choice of a method adequate to the research concept.

1.2   Ontology of the organization

Today, organizations have no distinct boundaries. Perhaps the most important correlate of this observation is the category of stakeholders introduced by Freeman (1984) to economic analysis and management.[3] The stakeholder theory defines enterprise not as a legal instrument designed to achieve the goal of earning profit for a select group of shareholders but as a social actor, and therefore can be perceived as an alternative theory of the firm. The firm is understood as a node of relationships between various stakeholders, a set of multilateral contracts, and an organization used by those various stakeholders to achieve their goals. As soon as the interwar period began, Berle and Means (1932) observed that corporations should no longer be understood as legal structures used by individuals to complete business transactions but as instruments in organizing economic life which due to their importance and proportions should be recognized as principal social institutions. Freeman continues this line of thought and argues that when corporations are conceived as principal social institutions, no special relationship between shareholders and directors exists. The belief has to be reviewed that managers are bound to further only the rights and interests of shareholders due to their ownership of the company. Such a view has to be changed to reject the 'managerial capitalism' concept that attributes the central importance to directors' loyalty towards shareholders, as emphasized in the agency theory, despite criticism of its various interpretations (Heath, 2009), and replace it with a new concept wherein managers are conceived as fiduciaries of a significantly larger group of stakeholders. Stakeholders include those individuals and groups that benefit or lose due to an organization's activity, and their rights can be either respected or violated by that activity. Importantly, the concept 'stakeholder' is a generalization of the term 'shareholder'. Also, stakeholders have their claims and expectations against firms. The nature of these claims is complex; they can be contradictory and can frequently require mediation. Stakeholders are much more diverse than the group of shareholders (Achterkamp & Vos, 2008). Since fundamentally different entities were included in the set of stakeholders, such as media, local and central authorities, religious organizations, civil movements, environmental and consumer organizations, and international organizations, the need arose to find a method of defining the relationships between the corporation or firm and the vast community of stakeholders. Various concepts of stakeholder *relationship management* have been proposed (Ramachandran, 2019), with their classification and prioritization based on such indicators as the potential for cooperation, the potential for creating threat to the organization, the congruence of interests of the firm and its stakeholders, or finally the firm's position in the contact network. In our opinion, these concepts are formulated in response to a changed ontology of the organization. Another aspect of the ontology of the organization is created by the emergence of the virtual structures indicated in the introductory section, with their diverse components and rapidly changing number of participants. This reality is not fully developed, is still being formed, but has already conquered the world of business, and not only that of business. The existence 'in relation' with something and 'in relation' to something stands for a new 'networked' quality of the organization. Facebook, Google, Instagram, YouTube, Amazon, Allegro, LinkedIn, and dozens of similar virtual structures are continuously 'vibrating', and perhaps their growth is not as rapid as in their initial years, but their proportions measured by the number of participants are still impressive.[4] Are random samples drawn from fast-growing populations still purposeful? What population is to be described by generalized analysis results – the population from which a sample was drawn but which no longer exists, or the population that did not exist in its current form at the time of research but has included the population that we sampled? Studying fast-growing populations poses a challenge, even if statisticians have developed methods to resolve a paradox of this type. The estimation, inference, forecasting, and trend analysis methods have been used for years. However, doubts remain. The changed ontology of the organization – the point of fundamental importance – presents a challenge to the conventional methodology of social sciences and management studies. The third important aspect of the ontology of the organization results from a change of perspective on defining society. Society today is distinct from that in the early Industrial Age or in antiquity. Sociologists argue that stable social structures have been replaced by transitory, fluctuating, variable 'social events', 'figurations' (Elias, 2007), 'structurations' (Giddens, 1984), or the 'social becoming' of society (Sztompka,

1991). Society is understood as a continually changing, fluctuating field of social events where individuals take mutual, culturally defined actions to create, modify, or remove social systems and groups and various elements of culture. Current reflection on management seems to ignore this changed perspective on perceiving society. How are organizations positioned in the field of social events? Can organizations become fields of events, and how? If they can, what are the consequences for organization management? Is integration possible in such a 'world of organizations'? Coordination? Hierarchy? Communication? Using what means? Multiple questions of this type arise, possibly suggesting that we are now facing a considerable change in our approach to management theory and practice.

1.3   Metamorphoses of knowledge

Knowledge had and has today multiple forms, dimensions, and aspects (Renn, 2022). Individual knowledge is based on remembered and encoded experiences, enabling an individual to solve problems through adaptive behaviour. We are capable of directing our attention to our experiences and correcting our individual knowledge, guided by the observed consequences of our behaviour. Knowledge can also be stored in the form of mental cognitive structures and reconstructed for new purposes or needs. The structure and content of knowledge are not separate. Each use of a structure – for example, recollecting the images of trees recorded in memory to recognize a tree seen for the first time – may lead to a change in knowledge content, complementing knowledge by a new image of a tree. Cognitive structures enable us to act also in situations where our information is incomplete. We refer then to implicit assumptions that allow recognition of an object, property, behaviour, or thing, or at least its assigning to a category or class. This function is served by stereotypes (Snyder et al., 1977; Bigler & Liben, 2006; Gelman & Roberts, 2017).

Certainly, knowledge has not only individual but also a social and material dimension. It may be shared with others, stored, and transmitted from generation to generation through symbolic systems, such as language. It may also be expressed and stored using material or immaterial devices – for example, in the form of digital records. *Scientific knowledge* has additional, special characteristics. It not only includes theory but also cultural practice or a series of cultural practices. It has emerged in developed societies in which the demand for knowledge did not result from merely pragmatic reasons. However, scientific knowledge is available in its 'fragmented' portions due to research specialization, publication rules, commercialization, and a number of other factors. They may hinder knowledge integration and implementation and prevent urgently needed innovation. High hopes for a change in this status have been raised by the Web revolution. The emergence of an epistemic Web will turn not only the content but also the system of links into a publicly available resource. In an epistemic Web, scientific knowledge would be directly accessible, identifiable, and suitable for assessing (Hyman & Renn, 2012). This level of transparency would promote trust in science and open new possibilities for cooperation between researchers and multiple other social groups.

Certainly, knowledge has a considerably long history. Initially, it was strictly local, related to the place of its origins. This refers to magical knowledge acquired by a clan or tribe. Knowledge today is also local, especially in those situations where sharing knowledge is excluded for the sake of state security, patent protection, or trade secrets. In time, knowledge set out on its 'journey', moving from one location to another – this movement resulted not only from economic development but also from Church missions combined with its economic activity. A fundamental role in distributing knowledge was performed in the past by monks who travelled from their home monasteries to distant countries. They disseminated knowledge and technology, including the knowledge of management.[5] Basically, knowledge is created by combining and integrating various concepts, and these processes have to be supported by social interaction and interdisciplinary cooperation. The exchange of knowledge across scientific disciplines may influence the evolution of culture and language and drive innovation and the development of science, not necessarily in a unidirectional, linear way (Sun & Latora, 2020).[6]

In view of the comments presented above, what is the status of knowledge of the organization and management processes? This knowledge, like that accumulated in other disciplines, has always resulted from the exchange of thoughts and observations, assumptions, critical judgement of concepts proposed, and from testing hypotheses or models – the exchange that was limited to the academic community for a long time. We know today for certain that knowledge suitable for management purposes is also created outside the world of the academy. It is developed in companies, in laboratories operated by large corporations that can frequently afford to hire the finest minds and expect commercialization of their research results. The group of holders and originators of knowledge that is crucial for management includes university lecturers, researchers on the organization and organizational processes, with the addition of consumers, raw material, and semi-finished product suppliers, distributors, sales force, prospective managers and line operatives, active participants in the organizational game as well as those who have quit it to retain experience and take a position of observers who perceive reality from the perspective of its dynamics and change. Observation of those groups and individuals in action reveals emergent knowledge, 'arising' from a complex network of links and human interaction. The most important conclusion drawn from the discussion outlined above reads that knowledge is created today in a complex network of agents (stakeholders) with their emotions, experience, feelings, aesthetic associations, stereotypes, everyday theories, and theories that are still developed following strict traditional methodology. This characteristic of knowledge as an emergent of interaction may not be ignored because it leads to improving products and services, serves customization of market offers, and – indirectly – is used in building a competitive advantage.

1.4 Change in methodology

In popular opinion, scientific research is aimed at extending knowledge. More precisely, it consists of the systematic search for data related to a question, problem raised. Scientific research is meaningful if it gives answers to new, not previously addressed questions, provides new data that confirm or falsify hypotheses, and reveals previously unknown relationships between various phenomena and processes. Research in this meaning may be described as 'a journey from the known to the unknown'. Traditionally, the distinguishing features of a research method include objectivity and systematicity. Objectivity requires the researcher to 'suspend' in the research process individual values, prejudices, beliefs, ideology. Can researchers, and how and when, 'suspend' their beliefs and worldview? Perhaps the best-known position was taken by Max Weber. He argued that science should 'free itself' from value judgements, science might not be used to legitimate any goal of action, and science should not indicate objectives to be achieved by humans. The results achieved by science may only be evaluated from the perspective of logic and the rules governing research procedure as recommended by the general methodology of research and not, for example, from the perspective of an ideology (Weber, 1999). The Weberian solution to the dilemma 'evaluate or not evaluate' is not universally accepted. Its critics argue that 'value-free science' (Lekka-Kowalik, 2010, p. 338) as proposed by Weber is not only impossible but also dangerous. Attention was directed to other dilemmas and their solutions intended to attain, at least partly, the ideal of value-free science. One of them arises from distinguishing 'internal' and 'external' components of science. The first category includes formulating theories and verifying hypotheses, and the other includes putting problems-questions and selecting methods. It was concluded that values may influence the 'external components' but not the structure of theory and the testing of hypotheses. The illusory foundation of this conclusion was indicated by T. Kuhn, who argued that it could be acceptable only if a means existed to undoubtedly distinguish between 'the internal' and 'the external'. Value judgements play an inevitable role in theory choice: they indicate what theory should belong to science and what is out of science (Kuhn, 1985). Putting aside other aspects of the debate on value reference, we wish to give attention to a theory developed in 1994–2003 by three authors: H. Nowotny, P. Scott, and M. Gibbons (2003). The authors propose a hypothesis saying that both 'the production of knowledge' and 'the process of research' have been 'radically transformed' by abandoning the old paradigm wherein a hierarchical system of disciplines was combined with the great importance of autonomy enjoyed by scientists and universities and adopting a new paradigm in which 'socially distributed, application-oriented, trans-disciplinary' knowledge is created in multiple places, not necessarily universities. Consequently, research activity and science can no longer be treated as 'the single epistemological ideal' of a neutral view and an objective investigation of the social or natural world. Instead, another understanding of research must be adopted: as a dialogue between various 'stakeholders' who contribute their perspectives to the research process. The role of those various stakeholders, including researchers, authorities, non-academic experts, media people, business practitioners, such as entrepreneurs and managers, or simply active citizens, is growing because research is conducted and 'knowledge is generated within the context of application' – knowledge is to serve people and society, contribute to development, and be 'socially robust' (Nowotny et al., op. cit., p. 179–194). Academics have no monopoly on resolving these questions since their research topics must be negotiated. Consequently, the environment wherein the problem is addressed influences the choice of methods, the structure of research programmes, and the planned use of research results. Given that the definition of research topics has become close to a conversation with various stakeholders, value reference in science cannot be avoided. The postulate of 'systematicity' in scientific research seems to be less controversial. However, B. Godin indicates that the meaning of this concept also evolves. The current concept of 'systematic' research is different from what it was decades ago. The author observes that the meaning of 'systematic' has drifted from an emphasis on the scientific method to an emphasis on institutionalized research. Godin (2001) argues that today 'systematic' means 'regulated' or 'planned', frequently in research organizations, but also in economic and political ones. Currently, the systematicity of research is associated with other characteristics than in the past. This results to a significant extent from the requirements of comparative statistics in research and development and from the concentration of funds for research in large organizations, such as the European Commission.

Methodological choices made in the search for truth and in the knowledge generation process are frequently determined by the view on the nature of surrounding reality, on the position of the researcher, and on the desirable role of the university in that reality, leading to specific intellectual decisions. Understood literally, the view is a matter of aesthetic reception, visual perception in this case, meaning the choice of such research material that by engaging the sense of sight allows to disclose an emotional perception of the reality under study – a perception that in our opinion can be an element of enhancement.

Notes

1. The term 'knowledge-based economy' suggests that today's economy is somehow fundamentally distinctive while economy has always been based on knowledge, even if not necessarily a scientific one; perhaps the

distinguishing feature of today's knowledge-based economy or knowledge-based organization consists only in the role played now by the pace of commercializing knowledge, embodying it in products and services, or the speed of transferring cutting-edge scientific discoveries to production.

2. For example, the experience of double socialization in various ethnic groups or experiencing tragic events of war.

3. However, the term *stakeholder* was first used in an internal memorandum at the Stanford Research Institute in 1963. This is described by Freeman et al. (Freeman & Reed, 1983).

4. For detailed data on this topic, see the portal https://backlinko.com/social-media-users#social-media-usage-stats (28.08.2023).

5. Wherever the Cistercians arrived, they arranged flour mills, waterwheel blacksmith's workshops, fish ponds, apiaries, breweries, and ironworks (e.g. in Szczyrzyc near Kraków, the Cistercians launched a brewery in 1628). Similar contributions were made by other monks, pilgrims, soldiers, merchants, settlers, or students who learned in schools throughout Europe.

6. Ye Sun and Vito Lattora made an analysis of knowledge transfer among different fields of physics to conclude that the highest levels of mutuality in the periods under study (1990–2000–2010) took place about 2000 and decreased in the following years. The method employed by the authors to investigate knowledge transfers in networks as a function of time demonstrated that significant discoveries in physics may influence other fields of physics and science even over long periods, and the patterns of knowledge sharing can evolve (Sun & Latora, 2020).

2 Constructing research programmes

Methodological requirements

The original methodological proposal underlying this study refers to the three findings previously discussed: (a) we observe a change of the mode of existence of the organization, (b) knowledge is currently available and generated in various places, not only at universities – a considerable portion of knowledge used in organizations is emergent by its nature, (c) the processes of knowledge generation and creation, testing, application, storing, finding, extending, or updating take place today in a complex interactive environment, while digital technologies make that interactivity permanent, not limited to the time of scientific congresses, conferences, or symposia.

2.1 Elementary research situation

We recognize that the primary source of research concepts lies in an individual mind, its resources, record of experience, memory of literature read and heard, lectures given by teachers, conversations with colleagues engaged in research work, conversations with other people. The statement that mind is the primary source of knowledge is thus a simplification, since mind is a record of everything encountered by an individual during their lifetime. All things recorded in mind undergo constant consolidation that consists in combining, classifying, dividing, processing, and assessing various 'entries'. These processes lead to the formation of knowledge. That knowledge is not completely certain; it is frequently hypothetical and contains statements that have to be confronted with data from multiple sources. It is also certain to an extent and contains a set of verified statements. It is almost always incomplete and stimulates to ask new questions to find gaps in the existing individual resource. That knowledge also sadly leads to developing schemata of response to the surrounding world and situations that we encounter, including habitual or stereotypical perception of reality, and a similar approach to knowledge and research. In this initial phase of research, it is advisable to adopt the approach proposed by phenomenology, especially its first method, known as 'the method of perceiving and describing what and how is given' (Krokos, 1998). This procedure aims to observe

DOI: 10.4324/9781003497103-3

in a phenomenon the property to be asserted. Observation, so understood, is intended to ensure source-oriented and neutral study: an absolutely unbiased attitude, to the exclusion of any a priori assumption. Observation focuses on both 'what' is given and 'how' it is given, and thus on the object as such and on the way the object is given. Cognition is understood here, to use a definition proposed by Ingarden, as actively deriving the meaning from the object, with emphasis put on the cognitive act and not on 'creating' the object (Krokos, 1998). What is given and how it is given, revealed by observation, have then to be described using direct concepts that must be 'learned' from observation. Thus, we have to suspend our knowledge of the object and turn our attention to the object again, being ready to perceive it free of any presupposition. The task is very difficult but must be performed to reduce the risk of repeated falling into mental habits in research. When considering their research purposes, all researchers are initially alone, without personal assistance from anyone, only with their individual body of knowledge, supported by a home archive consisting of a library or internet connection. This can be termed latent knowledge; we all have that knowledge – it is our individual property.

2.2 Dialogue

An idea, if not disclosed to others, one's community, friends, other people, discussed and criticized, will probably be abandoned. It will be put in the bin, possibly containing numerous similar abandoned projects. The decision to disclose the idea and encourage a conversation and discussion on its merits opens another crucial part of the knowledge creation process, namely dialogue. Dialogue (from the Greek διάλογος, *dialogos*, conversation) is a form of exchanging arguments between individuals in the spirit of cooperation, based on asking questions and giving answers to inspire critical thinking and reveal ideas and their underlying assumptions. Dialogue is probably the only method of study that is intended to *generate*, *test*, and *improve ideas*. No other method of study serves these three functions combined. Dialogue may take various forms. Let us consider, following the propositions put forward by two Japanese authors, I. Nonaka and H. Takeuchi (2000), the role of dialogue in the knowledge creation process. They discuss four knowledge conversion processes, referring them to knowledge creation in organizations. The first process consists of socialization – that is, sharing and creating knowledge through direct experience, for example, reading or conferences. This process is aimed at creating tacit knowledge, for example, in the form of mental models and technical know-how. This usually takes place in the everyday activity of an individual in a social context – the work environment, school, studio, or laboratory, as part of incidental or targeted observations of actions taken and speeches given by others. Dialogue provides an important means of socialization – it allows observing reactions of the interlocutor, discovering how thoughts are verbalized, tracing the references to reading and theories, remembering the moments of doubt and uncertainty. It consists of following the partner's line of thought, putting forward personal suggestions as to how to overcome the difficulties encountered. Importantly, the process may not be limited to criticism and must include proposing constructive ideas. The second conversion process consists of externalization – that is, articulating personal tacit knowledge using available concepts. Tacit knowledge is revealed through metaphors, analogy, hypotheses, and models. Externalization is activated by dialogue. This is the most important knowledge-creation process, as the source of new ideas is based on tacit knowledge. Combination refers to organizing ideas and including them in a specific knowledge system, consisting of explicit knowledge components, and selecting, categorizing, systematizing information with the aim of creating new knowledge. Also in this process, dialogue is irreplaceable, at least in the initial phases of work, research approach, and research topics. Dialogue enables us to make an initial balance, to estimate what we know of a topic and what remains unknown, to define the directions of study and the conditions for accepting new ideas. The participants in dialogue refer in this phase of work to their personal resources of explicit knowledge. The last knowledge conversion process distinguished, internalization, consists in embodying explicit knowledge into tacit knowledge – or in other words, in 'learning by doing'. The process of converting explicit knowledge to tacit knowledge is supported by the contents of documents, charts, and textbooks. Documents are useful for internalizing our experiences. However, the role of dialogue is irreplaceable also in this process: verbal accounts of events, descriptions of experiments, explanations, and illustrations given by interlocutors – all these confirm the importance of dialogue in internalizing explicit (available) knowledge.

2.3   Debate

Debate is a 'multiplied' dialogue form. Dialogue in its pure version refers to interaction between two people. Dialogue is intended to reveal tacit knowledge held by the interlocutors and convert it into an explicit message. Debate is the exchange of thoughts between more than two people who represent similar, or preferably different, types of professional experience. Debate goes a step further compared to dialogue, as a debate involves a greater number of participants and is usually conducted before an audience who can also speak. Debate enhances the perspective of elementary dialogue, usually expanding or complementing that perspective with the addition of new aspects or facts. This is especially true when a debate involves people who represent a variety of professional experience. The knowledge creation process carried out to write this book included debates with the participation of representatives of the academic community who professionally conduct research on organizations and management processes and of practitioners who use their knowledge in resolving actual decision-making problems, frequently with a complex structure. The cognitive process in a debate is closer to focused discussion sessions (focus group) than to brainstorming. Participants in a debate refer to each other's statements, developing theses proposed by former speakers, presenting critiques or new formulations of those theses, sharing examples from personal experience. The outcome of a debate may include new research questions and hypotheses, revealed correlations between events, and alternative perspectives on perceiving a single phenomenon. These results may provide a starting point for another stage of using the proposed method.

However, it can also happen that possibilities will open up embedded in sources previously underestimated in research on management. We refer here to works of art: literature, painting, photography.[1]

The final phase of the described procedure consists of designing, based on experiences acquired as part of dialogue and debates, a research project characterized by an approach to the topic which is new in its assumptions, although drawing from the achievements of qualitative analysis methods in its analytic aspect.[2]

The original programme of meetings designed by Barbara Fryzeł and titled 'Organizational Dialogues', which was initiated on 18 January 2023, provided a forum for the exchange of thoughts that allowed to develop a model procedure that can be termed 'parallel dialogues'.

Parallel dialogues, as depicted in Figure 2.1, take place both in the institutional sphere and between co-authors. The institutional aspect is aimed at

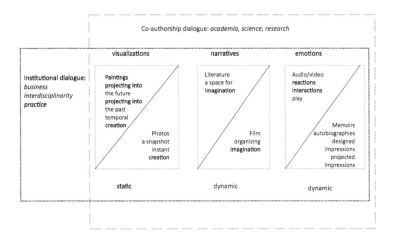

Figure 2.1 Parallel dialogues as a method of analysis

Source: Authors own elaboration

considering the practical, business perspective and seeing the topics under study in a way going beyond the narrow framework of a single discipline. This aspect complements the academic dialogue that is fundamentally research-oriented. An institutional dialogue relaxes academic rigour and supplements it with elements of digression, which are valuable because a free conversation reveals a variety of nuances that could be overlooked in the course of traditional reasoning that follows the convention of addressing those research questions that arise from literature review.

The intersection of practical and academic and research perspectives, complemented by interdisciplinary reflection on the organizational reality, opens a view on the representations of business and its agents in popular messages and narratives received by the public. We are thus interested in the visualizations of the world of organizations and business as recorded in pictures, works of art, and photographs, regarding a static approach. This part of reflection naturally leads to dynamic representations where a static depiction is replaced with a motion picture, a medium that organizes imagination, and a literary narrative that opens space for imagination. From visualizations to narratives, our line of thought aims at reflection on emotions and their role in the world of organizations and management – a role that is apparently reflected in material that records various business meetings and provides a basis for analysing the complexity of interaction, together with reminiscences, memoirs, autobiographies, distinct from other literary narratives in presenting personal engagement and attitude towards the reality described.

The subject matter of this book is the first research area indicated above: the visualizations of the business world and representations of topics related to that world in paintings and photographs.

2.4   Narratives: towards a synthesis

Analysis is not an ultimate objective of the research procedure that we adopt. The objective is to give a synthesis, and all we have said has served its preparations. An analysis crowns quantitative research. In qualitative research or research inspired by the methodology of art studies, another objective must be set. Analysis is an intermediate step on a way towards synthesis. Analysis invariably involves the deconstruction and decomposition of an object that undoubtedly exists as a natural and integral entirety; synthesis is a journey in the opposite direction, recombining divided and separately considered elements or components. This inductive procedure is our version of a scientific journey to explaining the picture of management.

In a specific data set that contains aesthetic, artistic objects, we seek, by dialogue, inspiration to discover the world of organizations, with the processes and events taking place in that world. Our research material includes photographs of prominent businesspeople, pictures referring to the condition of humans in a world dominated by large corporations, pictures capturing moments in organizational routines, 'bearing' styles of organization members, an industrial landscape intruding once-idyllic retreats, a landscape literally driving out nature from the town population's view. In processing this rather non-standard research material, we will not confine ourselves to working on the initial assumptions, exploring initial research topics, and using the conceptual framework of the first structure of codes deductively based on the literature and on analytic operations with their results presented in Section 4.1, '(De)coding the meanings of an aesthetic message'.

We also contemplate in private the works that give us inspiration. We confront with them our imagination and sensitivity, with the aim of discovering what was considered by their authors sufficiently important to be recorded in their pictures or photographs. We then meet in dialogue, exploring our personal ways of interpretation and searching for answers to the question, 'What have we learned about the organization and organization management from the same works perceived by each of us from an individual point of view?' The goal of recombining into their entirety those elements that were separated by the process of analysis can be achieved by replacing abstract dimensions with a narrative. A narrative or story joins together again the components that previously were analysed separately. We construct our narratives using another, namely the inductive and emergent structure of codes that we have identified in the process of analysis, talking about the represented individuals, situations, or events portrayed as a reality, an abstraction, a projection, or a simple illustration; the outcome is presented in Section 4.2 'Organizational tales'.

We hope that our journey through the material described will enable us to complement the knowledge of management with threads contributed by the visual imagination of artists who experience the organized world in their unique way.

Notes

1. The associated prospects are based on the achievements of visual sociology (Pauwels, 2010). Visual sociology is considered today a sub-discipline of its parent field of study, focusing on the visual dimension of social reality and material created by the participants in social life who document occurrences attracting their interest in their environment or regarded as worth recording. Also, sociologists can create their photographic or video archives documenting various social situations, for example, holiday celebrations, conflicts, social protests, arrangements of working spaces. These and other photographic records of events can give valuable insights into the values and actions of society members.

2. If necessary, return to a more traditional way of project designing is possible, with research project phases identified, heuristic models built, precise research questions specified, the type of plan defined, research methods selected, along with methods used to process and interpret data obtained, but that return is not always purposeful. Research may be complete with dialogue and debates, if they provide the project authors with data that is sufficient in their opinion.

3 Methodology of visual experiences and dialogue on the arts

The turn towards non-discursive methods of data acquisition has a wider dimension and is not limited to sociology or cultural anthropology. Jari Martikainen writes that towards the end of the 20th century, scholars in various fields of science started to challenge the dominant position of discursive research methods based on verbal material. That turn was motivated by recognizing the inadequacy of positivist methodology in the analysis of visual, sensory, and emotional experiences. The focus shifted towards developing and applying arts-based research methods aiming to complement the understanding of the social world provided by discursive research methods (Martikainen, 2018, 2019). Cole and Knowles (2008) write that arts-informed research aims to acknowledge

> the multiple dimensions that constitute and form the human condition –
> physical, emotional, spiritual, social, cultural – and the myriad ways of
> engaging in the world – oral, literal, visual, embodied. That is, to connect
> the work of the academy with the life and lives of communities through re-
> search that is accessible, evocative, embodied, empathic, and provocative.
> (Cole & Knowles, 2008, p. 60)

In arts-based research practices, a series of terms have been proposed that suggest certain shades of interest among the researchers using those methods – for example, a/r/tography, art as inquiry, art-based inquiry, artistic inquiry, or arts-informed research (Leavy, 2015, 2018). Martikainen argues that 'arts-based research' is an overarching term referring to these diverse concepts (Martikainen, 2019, p. 1).

In the field of management and organization analysis, arts-based research covers a wide scope of sources, such as drawing, painting (Mannay, 2010; Martikainen, 2018, 2019), photography, video recordings (LeBaron et al., 2018; Shortt & Warren, 2017), dance, and creative movement (Biehl-Missal & Springborg, 2015). Research conducted by Jari Matikainen, quoted above, was focused on such topics as employees' perception of leaders, organization members' conceptions of their

DOI: 10.4324/9781003497103-4

organization, and wicked problems in organizational life. Visual data (pictures, photographs from media) also provide material for participants to discuss topics that are interesting to the researcher. It follows from the last conclusion that visual methods are not intended to replace discursive ones but rather to complement verbal accounts collected in the research process and sometimes encourage participants to voice their opinion.

The methodological suggestion of using painting, photographs, videos, or drawings in social research is not exhaustive regarding possible inspirations from the arts. Verena Komander and Andreas König observe that management and organization scholars have long been intrigued by the performing arts, such as dance, music, and theatre. A connection established between the performing arts and performance in organizations has demonstrated that management, innovation, leadership, and other organizational phenomena have much in common with such activities as performing, directing, choreographing, and conducting (Mangham, 1990). The interest in these topics grew after the 1998 special issue of *Organization Science*, dedicated to jazz improvisation and organization theory. Komander and Konig (2022) indicate the benefits from referring to the performing arts in research on the world of organizations and encourage scholars to advance organizational theory by studying organizational phenomena in performing arts contexts. Important points in this set of topics include

- a contribution to the knowledge of 'social identity', where values are particularly important for stage artists and stakeholders in performing arts organizations that need to adapt their external communication in ways that may contradict their deeply held norms and values to acquire economic resources (Voss et al., 2000),
- a contribution to the knowledge of processes known as the *social construction of reality*, illustrated by research on how creative workers socially construct meaningfulness and try to reconcile meaningfulness with the economic instrumentality of work (Riza & Heller, 2015), and research on the social process of constructing aesthetics, illustrated by the idea that the organization process is a matter of art rather than science (Barnard, 1983),[1]
- a contribution to the knowledge of assessment and decision-making processes, for example, in the context of analysing how audiences assess the level of orchestral performance in terms of artistry, authenticity, and creativity, depending on the type of material received: sound-only, video-only, or video-plus-sound recordings; the research project demonstrated that the assessment was based primarily on visual rather than auditory cues (Tsay, 2013),
- a contribution to the knowledge of 'practice communities', such as theatrical groups, orchestras, string quartets, and portraying the conduct of leaders aimed at creating a climate for collaboration across and between the cast (Kramer & Crespy, 2011).

The performing arts are also used in advancing organizational theory by analysis of theatrical performances and corporate theatre (Clark & Mangham, 2004, p. 37), revealing sense-making and sense-giving processes in organizations (Cronin, 2008).

The arts are helpful in understanding organizational phenomena, especially

* understanding perception in and around the organization[2]
* understanding leadership.[3]

The arts-informed perspective is helpful in studying mental models and representations, as shown by K. E. Weick in his paper on improvisation as a mindset for organizational analysis (Weick, 1998).

Finally, the performing arts contribute to developing theories of organizational learning and memory; this strand of research identifies the best practices that developed in jazz improvisation and improvised theatrical performances to better understand and support the processes of learning, repeating, and imitating specific rules that eventually are used by organization members to develop their own repertoire of skills or to create completely new patterns (Barrett, 1998; Weick, 1992).

3.1   Aesthetics of the organization

The aesthetic perspective allows to ask questions about the role of art and emotions in the perception of the organization, especially about the feelings related to work in a specific place, office, firm, about the representations and visualizations accompanying the experience of work, about intentional use of artefacts, objects, colours, or architecture in designing the work environment. It is a type of research philosophy that uses metaphors, poetics, myths, pictures, or sounds (Strati, 2009) to illustrate or shape the organization process and emotions accompanying its experience.

Today's organizations can be viewed through the prism of geometry, with their linear and flat structure (Witkin, 2009). The organization of part of the world around us as an enterprise and the associated roles and behaviours of its members can be interpreted as a performance and broadly understood theatre (Carr & Hancock, 2003), with analysis of colour as a medium of current and past processes of aestheticization and their economic or social implications, in which colour is of fundamental importance for creating material culture (Beyes, 2017, p. 1478).

Images can be used, as indicated in previous sections, in qualitative research as a source of data, for example, in the form of photographs presented during interviews to facilitate participants' recollection of their experiences (see Warren, 2010, for an example).

Organizational aesthetics can take the form of control, namely dress codes or corporate communication language (Witkin, 2009). As an aesthetic aspect of every situation in an organization, it can encourage forming trust (Baer et al., 2018), assuming that people variously respond to various situations and tend to assess the associated experience in aesthetic categories such as pleasing, beautiful, tasteful. Those assessments can have long-lasting effects on attitudes and behaviours, for example, purchasing decisions made by consumers or employee involvement and loyalty.

Aesthetic categories enhance the understanding of ethical topics, assuming that the intrinsic good is related to good experience, based on an aesthetic criterion, such as harmony (Hartshorne, 1974, p. 214). Thus, the categories of good or evil are reduced to the beautiful or ugly (Brady, 1986; Whitehead, 1938), raising the issue of justifying a line of thought where the beautiful and therefore good are also ethical (Hancock, 2005).

Richardson (2019) indicates the role of aesthetics in disguising the 'ugly' elements of organizational reality or strictly understood corporate practices. The author discusses the aestheticization of our world, exemplified by the visual appeal of shopping malls and the promotion of consumer culture (temples of consumption), and constructing a dissenting narrative about the world today – a narrative that is strengthened by celebrities and attractive to consumers but may be unreal to a certain extent (Richardson, 2019).

The aesthetic perspective of analysis so understood is seen in discourse on corporate social responsibility (CSR), introducing the term 'green illusions' referring to the phenomenon of aestheticization of CSR communications that blur the boundary between the real and the illusory and may be used to divert attention away from real problems and to present corporations in a better light than by revealing facts (Richardson, 2019).

On the one hand, the development of technology and digitalization set increasingly demanding requirements regarding such competences as innovation or creativity; on the other hand, the growing role of technocracy and the utilitarian aspect that prevails in assessing reality may lead to certain negligence of those areas of intellectual activity which are fundamental for creativity, namely imagination or experimenting.

To achieve a balance in view of the described phenomenon, disciplines are frequently combined in education, for example, theatre, visual arts, and business studies, to give students the chance to use extra-rational techniques, liberal arts methods (Beckman et al., 2018) (Homayoun & Henriksen, 2018). Various types of performances and art events serve as therapeutic techniques, for example in hospitals (Preston & Jean-Louis, 2020).

The multiple threads addressed in the debate on interrelations between the visual arts and the world of management, organizations, and business, methodological interdependence, cognitive analyses of art, and organizational analyses, especially the cognitive value of the indicated interrelations in which perception of the organization is revealed and recorded, enable us to bring up key questions that will be examined and answered in this book.

- What perception of the world of organizations and business is transmitted using the visual arts of painting and photography?
- How do the aesthetic canons accepted in an age/style/picture type correspond with a change in the perception of business/businesspeople?

In an analysis of works dedicated to the subject matter of business, entrepreneurs, or companies, it may be reasonably assumed that the works convey specific mindsets of their authors, serving representations of opinions prevailing in their age, community, or society, that is, exemplify or express their idiosyncrasies to evoke in the receiver an intended response, reflection, or emotion. Following this line of thought, an analysis of the indicated works gives answers to the questions about both the image of the world of organizations as reflected in art and the role of art in the intentional shaping of that world.

3.2 Content in visual objects

Our schemes for interpreting visual works are inspired by canonical, in a sense, studies on content analysis (Berelson, 1952) and on fundamental concepts in the history of art that allow to reveal the universal rules and mechanisms leading to creating beauty (Wölfflin, 2015).

Content analysis is a research technique for the objective, systematic description of the content of communication (Berelson, 1952), considering observations and evaluation of the symbolic content of communication (Kolbe & Burnett, 1991), both written and visual. The concept of content analysis may also be applied to works of art.

Inspired by the approach rooted in grounded theory (Glaser & Strauss, 1967), we complemented certain previously defined codes by inductively creating open codes that reflect new themes that were not considered before, which frequently occurs in the case of coding comprehensive material on a topic poorly examined in the literature (Rubin & Rubin, 2005), especially visual material, opening a considerably wider space for interpretation. While open, inductive categories were only supplementary in the first coding phase, and that part of the analysis was aimed principally at interpreting aesthetic material according to the existing, recognized convention of content analysis, our approach in the second phase was purely exploratory, based on dialogue and the inductive definition of semantic categories, and its outcome consists of narratives and organizational tales that we constructed.

The categories used to code contents of pictures understood as messages include such characteristics as the subject matter of the message, for example an individual, group, event, but also an organization or institution, and the vector of the message that may indicate neutral, favourable, or unfavourable treatment of the subject matter. In open coding, we complemented the category of subject matter of communication by process, habitat, and environment. The analysis covered the physical and personality features of individuals depicted in messages and an active or passive attitude of the author. Meaningful pieces of content also include (possible) stereotypes, values, a form of authority captured, and the way of portraying that authority. The type of message objective also seems to be of key importance: reflective, emotional persuasive, or exemplifying, which can be manifest in visual works.

We consider the sense transfer methods used in a message to be particularly important as they open a large space for interpretation; Aleksander Marcinkowski has complemented the original list of units of analysis[4] proposed by Berelson (1952) by additional categories of sense transfer:

- by opposition – that is, by indicating concepts or pictures that convey conflicting meanings, anti-models, contrasts,
- by subsumption or exclusion – that is, by accepting or excepting a meaning in/from a wider set of referents, for example representing a figure as the epitome of a social category, an example of a 'social type', or showing an individual, organization, situation as 'marginal', excepted, estranged, excluded,[5]
- by context – that is, by showing that a concept, figure, or group exists among others, in a relationship with the environment or objects seen in the picture or photograph, and thus introducing elements of relational analysis,
- by correlation – that is, by presenting concepts, images, figures or situations that are related, connected, similar in meaning or synonymous, the similarity of postures or gestures,
- by exegesis – that is, by showing the past meaning of a figure, building, interior, reminding or indicating the importance of an object or individual in a commendable or blameworthy sense,
- by strictly understood exemplification – that is, by indicating examples of the situation described, visualization of the history, important events, people performing typical tasks, wearing period clothes.

Considering the specific nature of the topic of business, organization and management, with their visual and aesthetic representations as the subject of our study, we omit the coding of causes of a communication, originally proposed by Berelson, as inadequate for our research purpose, while we complement selected categories, whenever this is reasonable, in the coding process by open codes – this refers to the category of characteristics of figures portrayed in a message – and by categories defined on the basis of the existing literature on the subject – this refers to the codes related to values, where we use the existing typologies of competing values (Maher, 2000), and individual and organizational values considered from the perspective of their congruence (Liedtka, 1989). We transferred the coding of stereotypes, although they may seem obvious in the context of management and business, and referred to such matters as clothes worn by the figures portrayed (a suit), their accessories in the picture (documents, a fountain pen, telephone), or gender (the predomi-nance of men in pictures or a negative connotation in representing women) to the second coding phase. The final version of the codebook is contained in an attachment to this study. We adapted content analysis to visual works, in-cluding aesthetic categories in the analysis of visual material (Wölfflin, 2006, 2009, 2015).

Wölfflin (2006) suggests the existence of basic ideas – the most general representational forms – that he considers to be the element leading to beauty creation. He thus proposes an analytical scheme that allows an analysis of a work of art in its deepest essence, revealing a canvas on which idiosyncra-sies are built, reflecting a period style, a national style, or that of an ethnic group. Consequently, it is a scheme of certain original ideas that enables us to perceive differences in the way of arriving at specific representations and may bring into view what can be termed original assumptions in an analysis of organizational cultures. It can be argued for this reason that an interpreta-tion of a scheme defining representational forms reveals deep beliefs as to the nature of the themes represented – here, the world and people of organizations and business.

Those basic forms that we treat as dichotomies, opposite meanings, defin-ing space for interpretation of the tacit meaning assigned to organization and management objects, include (Table 3.1)

- linear versus painterly
- plane versus recession
- closed versus open form
- multiplicity versus unity
- clearness versus unclearness (of the object represented)

The linear in a work refers to focusing on a shape or form distinguished by clear contour while blurring such fixed boundaries between the objects and the background, and the focus on producing optical effects by a combination of colour patches is characteristic of a painterly work. In linear works, our sight follows a line, while the explicit depiction of distinguished solid forms makes them somehow perceptible by touch. The painterly approach shows solid figures in their connection with other picture elements, making them boundless, and focuses on optical reception, creating an effect by a composi-tion of patches. The consequence of a linear approach is that emphasis is put on a plane treated as a part of a line, while the painterly approach accentuates arrangement in space and seeks perspective.

Table 3.1 Basic concepts in picture analysis and views on the organization

Linear – painterly	*Aesthetics of views on the organization*
Sight follows a line – a holistic experience of an optical phenomenon	subsystem management – holistic management
The impression of tactility of solids – the impression of solids being boundless	organizational boundaries – fuzzy organization
Contours, planes, edges, boundaries – a light, subtle entirety, patches	individual success – success as a result of the synergy of actions taken by multiple agents
Value of single objects – objects interrelated in a unity	
Plane – recession	
Planar combination of constituents – uniform recession	hierarchy/flat/matrix structures – a spatial view on the organization
Sequence of separate layers – enormous foregrounds, space represented through patches	sequential order – multifunction teams
Contours parallel to the stage edge	
Plane as a part of line – foreshortening, imitation of movement, spatially arranged objects	
Maximum visibility of solids – sharp light contrast	
Closed – open form	
Congruency – flexible rules	mechanistic metaphor of the organization – biological/ organic metaphor
Staying within a framework – no limits	
An axis of symmetry – no axis	an integral organization – a virtual organization
The vertical/horizontal – axes and diagonals	
An autonomous world fragment – a fleeting moment	
Face and profile views, defined by a framework – figures at other angles than a framework	
Geometric representation (e.g. a circular halo)	
Uniform distribution of brightness on a plane – colour accents	
A 'building', 'architectural' style – variation/ liveliness	
Multiplicity – unity	
Single, distinct parts that are given their own lives (detail), preserving their identity – elements subordinated to the dominant theme	a fragmented view – structural causality autarky – autopoiesis
Clearness – unclearness	
Representing objects as they are individually (as many hand pairs as many figures) – phenomenal, holistic representation	formalism (e.g. procedures) – adhocracy
Representing single elements in their entirety – representing elements only by suggestion for sight	
Light and colour to define the form – light and form given their own lives	

Source: Authors own elaboration based on Wölfflin (2006)

The planarity of a work is expressed in a clear relative arrangement of objects depicted, frequently in stripes or rows, while a spatial organization of composition, in which various forms of perspective are used, results in the effect of recession, forcing the spectator to visually seek it, to 'immerse' in the work.

The closed form of a work makes it seem complete and fully contained within its framework – an effect produced by symmetry and adoption of a specific central point. The open form is characteristic of works that seem to reach beyond their framework and have no boundaries, which may result from using asymmetry.

Multiplicity refers to the independence and autonomy of individual depicted elements, each given 'a life on its own' in aesthetic terms. It can be imagined that a detail in this type of work could function as a separate and autonomous work of art. Unity means organizing the relationship between individual details so that they are justified by their co-existence and concurrence – they carry meanings in relation to each other and thus can be treated as constituents of a larger narrative that has its dominant, leading theme.

Consequently, clearness of a work refers to the focus on the form of individual elements, the form as such, fully represented by means of colour and light; unclearness is characteristic of works in which the artist offers the spectator only indicative points for sight while focusing on a phenomenal, holistic representation of an object.

In our search for representations of business figures and of the world of organizations in art, we decided to consider a series of works – paintings, graphics, photographs – selected from internet museum collections and auction catalogues, using such key words as *business, businessman, businessmen, business woman, organization, firm, enterprise.*

We included collection catalogues made available on the websites of The Metropolitan Museum of Art, The National Gallery, London, Musée du Louvre, Museo Nacional del Prado, Tate, Alte Nationalgalerie, J. Paul Getty Museum, The National Gallery of Art, Washington, and auction catalogues displayed by Christie's and Sotheby's.

The set of paintings and graphics subject to analysis consists principally of modern works from the 20th century (sixteen) and 21st century (one), but also of single works from historical periods (one work from the 16th century, three works from the 18th century, and one work from the 19th century). Importantly, regarding the historical and social context of the works, four of them date back to the period of the First World War or the time immediately after its end or from the Great Depression time. The context of a work is influenced not only by the temporal but also by the national aspect: it should be indicated that the set of pictures under study consists mainly of British and American works, including four created by artists who originated from other countries but migrated to and were active in the United States. Few works, mainly historical, were created in the Netherlands, France, or Germany.

The set of photographs that we analysed is more uniform. It consists of works by Walker Evans,[6] created mainly for *Fortune* magazine and representing key figures of American business. The set includes portraits of directors from Kaiser-Frazer's Automobile Plant (1946), McCollum[7] from Continental Oil (1952); portraits of bankers, for example Joseph Barr,[8] taken in 1950–1960; Vickers[9] from Sperry (1953); photographs of a representative of 3M (1951); Ganger from Lorillard[10] (1952); Craig from AT&T (1951); M. J. Rathbone from Jersey Standard Oil (1954); F. W. Ecker from Metropolitan Life (1953); Russell from Southern Pacific (1951–1952); Cordiner from General Electric (1952); McCloy from Chase (1953); Clifford F. Hood from U.S. Steel (1952); and works portraying business figures in street scenes, such as *Two Businessmen in Hats Talking on Street, Florida* (1941) or *Two Businessmen: for the Series 'Dress'* from 1963. We also included the works *Business Manager of a Theatre (Kaufmännischer Direktor eines Theaters)* done in 1930–1935 by August Sander[11] (1876–1964) from the collection of J.P. Getty Trust *Travelling Business Man, Rhineland (Reisender Kaufmann, Rheinland)* from 1930 and *Young Businessman* from 1927 by the same artist, and photographs from the Tate Gallery collection *London Stock Exchange, a Typical Young Businessman* by Emil Otto Hoppe.

Finally, we analysed 86 documents, including 61 photographs and 25 paintings. In sampling material for analysis, we also used a snowballing technique. For example, a set of works by Edward Hopper representing office scenes were included in our study after an additional search for works by this artist based on the first painting held by the Met. Visual material was collected between 21 May 2023 and 30 September 2023.

Research reliability in a qualitative approach is confirmed by the degree of agreement in the coding process carried out independently by coders, which must reach 80% or more in most situations (Lombard et al., 2002), but 70% may be appropriate in exploratory studies.

The reasons that in some situations prevent reaching a high level of inter-coder agreement include

- work on a complex code system while the literature fails to offer a reliable and pre-tested code system for a specific type of topic (Krippendorff, 2004);
- work with material that requires coding of more extensive paragraphs, or visual material as in our case, opening considerably wider space for idiosyncrasies and individual interpretations than a standard coding of phrases or short sentences, for example from an interview text (Weber, 1990);
- the varying graphic quality of the material to be coded.

Importantly, inter-coder agreement basically refers to situations where the code system is pre-defined and analysis is based on deduction (Campbell et al., 2013), while relatively limited evidence indicates how to address the question of agreement in an inductive procedure (Armstrong et al., 1997; Popping, 1992), with material coded using open codes that define certain emergent conceptual and semantic categories. The dialogue method employed in our study solves that problem, enabling us to negotiate an interpretation of material subject to analysis and to record that interpretation in the form of codes, subsequently aggregated to form higher-level categories.

We achieved inter-coder reliability of 71.39% for paintings and 72.90% for photographs, that is, an acceptable level in the case of exploratory research.

Content analysis is naturally connected with the formal analysis of a work of art, addressing, among others, the elements shown in Table 3.2.

From the perspective of our research topics: depictions of the world of organizations, it seems of key importance to understand how elements of art, composition, colouring, light and dark contrasts, or means of expression form representations, pictures of business themes, undoubtedly conveying an encoded understanding of business phenomena as seen by the work's author and providing a space where to locate certain meaningful motifs, attributes, or symbols.[12]

To summarize, we define initial analysis as a quantitative estimation of codes regarding the structure of basic content analysis categories, complemented by open codes (authority, figure traits, values), but treated as basically deductive. The analysis proper refers to the section where we deal with open

Table 3.2 Selected elements in work art analysis

Form	Composition, i.e. organization of space with all elements that fill it	axes, sections, directional tensions	composition: open/closed, tight/loose, dynamic/ static, diagonal/horizontal/ vertical, movement, horizon
	Colouring	colour use	wide/narrow colour scheme, rules of classical perspective: warm/cool hues, value/temperature contrasts, dominant
	Chiaroscuro	light distribution	the source of light, lighting/ dispersion degree, mood, impasto, form modelling
	Expression	means of expression	patch, line, illusionism/ realism, dramaturgy, symbolism, dynamics, drawing, proportions, perspective, harmony, balance, rhythms
Content	Iconographic aspects	motifs and themes	allegories, personifications, symbols, attributes
	Iconological aspects	contexts	work origins, cultural and social circumstances, and determinants

Source: Authors own elaboration based on Wölfflin (2006)

codes, emergent themes, and create our own narrative about representations of business in works of art.

The final phase in proposing an understanding of representations of the organizational world from the perspective of organizational aesthetics is to apply a filter of aesthetic impressions on the constructed organizational tales presented in section *Palaces and cathedrals*. . . . This can be done using selected categories contained in Table 3.2.

Probably, some of the distinguished aesthetic dichotomies accurately illustrate various research paradigms. For example, the concept of autonomy of individual parts constituting an entirety reminds of the positivist perception of objectively existing elements living their own separate lives, while a representational journey towards unity, assuming the appearance of a dominant element that in a sense justifies the existence of single constituents, by no means excludes an approach based on deductive thinking. The question of a work's clearness or unclearness requires other considerations: the latter can be associated with an inductive approach where we infer the existence of individual elements based on our view on the whole and the impression it generates by way of subtle hints and allusions. This is also a kind of phenomenological perspective, tending to represent objects in a phenomenal manner that, if characterized by particularism, may evoke associations with the idiographic approach in which our attempt to understand a particular phenomenon is based on the assumption that the phenomenon somehow represents a larger reality, although we have no reason to make generalizations.

3.3 Architecture of metaphors and associations

The performing arts offer us an option of seeing organizations that belong to a wider domain of organizational aesthetics – a research perspective that frequently relies on metaphors and poetics.

The arts and their aesthetic values carry a symbolic message that is particularly evident in architecture as the art of building and interior design. An analysis of the symbolic characteristics of buildings and spaces may reveal that they convey a message of power. This refers to buildings where the 'depth' of rooms occupied by specific people in the entire structure, be it CEO offices or state rooms in a palace, and the length of the way that guests have to go to meet those occupants are indicators of social status (Dovey, 1999; via Kerr & Robinson, 2016). This type of symbolic message of power is characteristic of many historical periods and is exemplified by the Palace of Versailles or, more recently, by the Ciudad Santander corporate complex (Kerr & Robinson, 2016). Like great monarchs, chief executives of financial institutions can have their private, 'back' stairs to their offices, a private lift, or a private entrance to the board meeting room, like to a palace chapel (Dovey, 1999). Offices occupied by executives, with luxurious interior design, specially designed furniture, decorated with artworks, and an 'executive kitchen' with service working round the clock, are frequently hidden in green areas and gardens separating the world of 'rules' from others, like on the corporate campus of the Royal Bank of Scotland (Bourdieu, 1993, p. 257; via Kerr & Robinson, 2016). Banks tend to adopt classical architectural styles, largely characterized by large, prominent columns emblematic of stability and strength, as exemplified by Gibson Hall with its Byzantine interior (Barnes & Newton, 2019) or the headquarters of the London and Westminster Bank, opened in 1838, utilizing Greek and Roman symbols (Black, 1996, 64) intended to convey commercial power (Conway & Roenisch, 2005, p. 181; via Barnes & Newton, 2019) and credibility.

The term 'cathedrals of consumption' was proposed in *Enchanting a Disenchanted World: Revolutionizing the Means of Consumption* by George Ritzer (1999).[13] He used it to describe a specific way of organizing commercial spaces that are both rationally arranged and have their enchanting qualities. They enchant consumers with their glamour, narrative, sometimes aesthetic, although they are designed to serve economically effective consumption in a highly rationalized and optimized manner to achieve maximum profitability. A visit to a shopping mall can thus meet the criteria of pilgrimage to a place where to meet others, feel a sense of community, partaking in a ceremony, and even connect with nature, due to the sometimes sophisticated interior design of this type of building or establishment. These places offer people similar emotions as festivals, provide communities with services, can be sources of spiritual experiences, thus assuming a quasi-religious character of space where undemanding customers can practise their worldly consumer religion (Ritzer, 2010).

The use of metaphors in the title of a set of organizational narratives that are to reflect the aesthetics and poetics of representation of business and the world of organizations is also inspired by insight into the analysed artworks that partly refer to the symbolism described above, with its canonical example: the painting by Stettheimer with the characteristic title *The Cathedrals of Wall Street*. The depicted space is dominated by the emblematic architecture of classical-style buildings with their harmonious, though overwhelming, and respectable facades that set a framework for the functioning of modern society and are worshipped by the correlated and interrelated spheres of politics and business.

Trade and finance are the key areas that can be identified with markets, economic systems, and, first of all, with organizations that constitute them. Financial institutions, banks, and their representatives occupy a prominent place in depictions of business, not only in the form of portraits of professionals representing this industry, but also symbolically. Trade is represented in the organizational depictions we analyse on the London, New York, and Paris stock exchanges. This specific architecture of associations provided key inspiration for the narratives and tales that we present in the following chapter.

Notes

1. New research projects conducted in this spirit illustrate how musical directors and leaders construct aesthetic leadership using their artistic practices (Ladkin, 2008).
2. For example, Biehl-Missal (2011) attended 40 annual general meetings, press conferences, and analyst meetings of German companies listed on the stock exchange. Inspired by performance theory (see Schechner, 2003), the author describes how companies employed lighting and other dramaturgical techniques to make audience members feel like passive spectators (at general meetings) or invoke a feeling of community (at analyst meetings).
3. This strand of research adopts the interactive perspective derived from dramaturgical theory (Goffman, 1981) in its attempts at describing leadership; it is suggested that leaders and their subordinates (followers) jointly construct a leader's authenticity, charisma, and fame while interacting (Gardner & Avolio, 1998; Jackson, 1996; Ladkin & Taylor, 2010).
4. The textbook by B. Berelson, codifying the content analysis method (*Content Analysis in Communications Research*. Glencoe: Free Press Publications), is not readily available on the internet. The reader will find a description of categories and units of content analysis as proposed by Berelson in a 1970 book published by the press research centre Ośrodek Badań Prasoznawczych RSW Prasa in Kraków (in Polish). The book is displayed at https://pm.media.uj.edu.pl/documents/19112558/0/Berelson+-+Analiza+zawarto%C5%9Bci.pdf/edb43b30-2820-4cb7-8f0e-a6d6e29c2130.
5. The category of exclusion has grown in importance as considered from the perspective of current social narratives. The close connection between private organizations or business and social problems of poverty, hunger, the right to adequate housing, or the right of access to fundamental public or consumer goods (the latter being more controversial) is constituted in corporate responsibility strategies, and this directly introduces the matter of various forms of exclusion in the catalogue of organizational goals (preventing exclusion, inclusive policies), consequently making inclusiveness an important organizational value (see Rehr & Zaniello, 2017).
6. Walker Evans (1903–1975) was a prominent American documentary photographer. His works, created in the convention of poetic journalism, represented products, artefacts, and the essence of American culture, portraying typical, exemplary scenes or figures of American life. His photographs show people captured in a fleeting moment, in ordinary, everyday life situations while landscapes, buildings, and architecture are depicted in an artistic convention of dominating structures, frequently approaching a kind of abstraction. That photography aimed at documenting typical daily life, iconic examples of a situation or community (this is evident in the series of photographs depicting business figures). In this sense, the art of Evans stood in opposition to the aestheticized strand of artistic photography proposed by Alfred Stieglitz, a modernist who in his art of photography tended to refer to painting (pictorialism) and to show the beauty of scenes or objects depicted, paying particular attention to recession, perspective, composition,

being far from documenting specific reality. Evans moved away from modernist aesthetic and turned to realism, which resulted in works that combine 'the nuance of a poet with the precision of a surgeon' (Department of Photographs. 'Walker Evans (1903–1975).' In Heilbrunn Timeline of Art History. New York: The Metropolitan Museum of Art, 2000–. www.metmuseum.org/toah/hd/evan/hd_evan.htm (October 2004, accessed: 11.08.2023).

7. Leonard F. McCollum (1902–1993) was president and chairman of Continental Oil Company (Conoco) for more than two decades (1947–1972), when he developed the company through multiple innovation projects and an aggressive international strategy. As a philanthropist, he founded, for example, the Executive Education Centre at Harvard Business School (McCollum Centre) (www.hbs.edu/about/campus-and-culture/campus-built-on-philanthropy/Pages/mccollum-center.aspx, accessed: 14.08.23).

8. Joseph W. Barr (1918–1996) was the US secretary of the treasury in President L. Johnson's the administration and then continued his career in banking in the position of chairman of Federal Home Loan Bank in Atlanta.

9. Harry F. Vickers (1898–1977) was an inventor who specialized in mechanics and hydraulic systems. He served as president of Sperry and then Sperry Rand Corporation.

10. Robert M. Ganger was portrayed by Evans as president of the P. Lorillard Co. tobacco company, a position that he occupied in the early 1950s to resign after a relatively short period (https://content.time.com/time/subscriber/article/0,33009,829288-5,00.html, accessed: 14.08.2023).

11. August Sander (1876–1964) was a German artist who, like Evans, aimed to depict the truth and document reality in his art. Conceptual and theoretical foundations of his photographs were provided by 'new objectivity' that sought to depart from abstraction and return to realism (Jane Pierce, August Sander, www.moma.org/artists/5145, accessed: 11.08.2023).

12. Content analysis of visual objects, mainly photographs, is present in the literature on business, for example, in the context of advertising material used in the tourism industry (Govers & Go, 2005). The conceptual framework may include in this case analysis of motifs and related objects photographed, especially the identification of objects depicted, their grouping, relationships with other depicted objects or artefacts, and the context in which they are captured (Sternberg, 1997). In this type of approach, completing a list of objects seems advisable to estimate the frequency of their appearance in the entire sample of analysed pictures and to eventually determine which of them and how often they appear together and in what context. In a sense, this approach is similar to the quantitative analysis method of encoded material implemented in the MAXQDA 2022 programme.

13. It is worth noting that Baudrillard speaks about similar context 30 years earlier, saying: 'Comme dans le Pantheon romain venaient syncretiquement coexister les dieux de tous les pays, dans un immense « digest », ainsi dans notre Super-Shopping Center, qui est notre Pantheon a nous, notre Pandemonium, viennent se reunir tous les dieux, ou les demons, de la consommation, c'est-a-dire toutes les activites, tous les travaux, tous les conflits et toutes les saisons abolis dans la meme abstraction' (Baudrillard, 1970, p. 26).

4 Palaces and cathedrals of finance, temples of trade

Paintings and photographs

4.1 (De)coding the meanings of an aesthetic message

4.1.1 Neutral similarities and reflective contexts

The first step in the present picture and photograph analysis was to develop a coding scheme of material for the purposes of content analysis (Berelson, 1952), partly complemented by open coding.

Considering the topic of communication (Chart 4.1), a substantial majority of pictures and photographs that depict the world of organizations consists of portraits of specific persons (71.3%) occasionally represented in a company (25.7%), thus forming a group, and more frequently posing, being thus rather passive (57.4%) than captured in a type of activity.

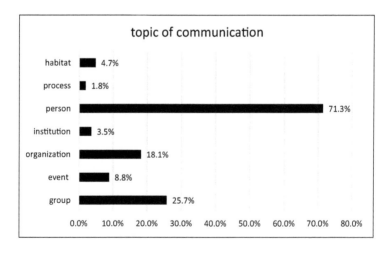

Chart 4.1 Structure of topics in communication

Source: Authors own elaboration

DOI: 10.4324/9781003497103-5

Although more than 80% of the depictions under study are used to representatively show certain social types, role models or members of a specific class – that is, to give exemplifications, there are not infrequent pictures or photographs that have a considerable potential of stimulating emotions and reflection in the receiver. The communication objectives so understood are shown in Chart 4.2.

It is hard to remain unmoved when seeing *Organizational Advances* by Albert Potter,[1] with its black and white, contrasted and depressing colour scheme, and the striking facial expressions of figures, moving chaotically, crowding a limited space, creating a powerful, distressing narrative.

Here we see a densely composed scene with a crowd of male figures carrying various commercial ads. A sad individual in a hat, with his eyes lowered and a droopy moustache, advertises stylish clothing, while his companion, equally frustrated, advertises loans. To the left, there are two figures in flat caps, one of them turning his back on the viewer, facing skyscrapers in the background that replace the horizon line, and carrying a board with a partly legible motto 'take your time'. The last word can be guessed from a visible fragment of a watch. The other figure, shown in profile, with a pipe in his mouth, carries on his back a board advertising footwear and lingerie. All figures have sunken cheeks and sharp facial features, but attention is mostly attracted by the figure in the left upper corner, with his haggard face – if considered an autonomous component of the work, it would be unclear whether that face belongs to a living or a dead man. This figure carries an advertising board that reads 'vitality'. The composition is dominated by a board, situated

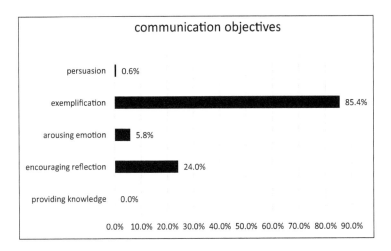

Chart 4.2 Structure of communication objectives

Source: Authors own elaboration

towards the back, but with enormous dimensions, advertising a beauty school and cosmetic products. The entire group seems to be pressed into a frame defined by a depiction of metropolis and business in the horizon and a kind of fence with a garbage can placed in the foreground.

The message, which seems to lampoon a market economy, indicates its negative aspects, and portrays shabby desperate figures who are still hired to advertise beauty products or elegant garments, is profoundly grim, negative. The feelings of frustration and depression are clearly recognizable in the faces of the figures who seem to impassively and automatically perform their disbelieved and indifferent tasks that are still necessary to earn income and survive in hard times.

Equally, emotional reaction is triggered by *Employment Office* by Gross-Bettelheim,[2] rendered in a contrastive, black and white colour scheme with sharp chiaroscuro.

Here, we see three figures standing in a line, one by one, with their forearms resting on a counter. They stand in a queue for chance, as the work title indicates: a man and a woman with depressed faces. Despite simplified drawing and sparing line style, depression is clearly indicated by drooping mouths. The horizontal wrinkles on the forehead of the first man correspond with his eyebrows drooping along a single line, augmenting the impression of absolute frustration and failure. The man in the middle seems to smile faintly and shyly – maybe he is the only one who still has hope or tries to win over a person standing on the other side of the counter, who is invisible to us, but may decide on offering a good job. Strong light falling from the top lamp with a bare bulb brings out of the dark almost white faces of the people waiting for something. Empathy may be aroused by the frustrated faces of people in hardship, and the sharp, sectional lighting of the space, reminding of a kind of detention, literal or metaphorical, may evoke the feeling or anxiety or even fear.

Both works are examples of pictures that provoke emotional response and simultaneously encourage reflection.

Considering the predominance of works with a neutral communicative direction, as shown in Chart 4.3, the two described works exemplify an unfavourable direction of communication.

Quite an opposite message is conveyed using completely different aesthetic means in the work by George Condo *The Businessman*, depicting a man with a Janus face whose one half, with mouth open in a scream of horror, or maybe aggression, can arouse equally anxiety and fear or even disgust. A balding individual in a suit combines two figures. The left part of his face includes a dilated, maybe with sudden fear, eye and an enormous mouth wide open in scream. The right side includes a calm eye and gentle contour of an eyebrow above. From this perspective, his mouth is invisible. It is replaced by an irregular solid gagging him. Certain aesthetic discomfort is also caused by the painting's colour scheme: the figure is portrayed on a bright orange

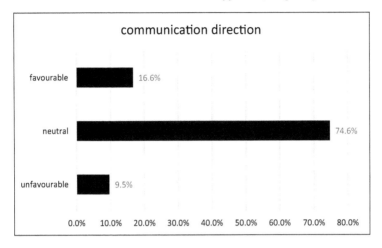

Chart 4.3 Structure of communication direction

Source: Authors own elaboration

background incongruous with his pink face complexion. This is balanced by a dark suit and tie.

This painting is a typical example of a message that is aimed not at exemplification but at evoking emotions, and a good example of how the purpose of a message can be connected with its direction – favourable, unfavourable, or neutral. *Businessman* by Condo is a work arousing emotions with an unfavourable direction of communication, where also symbolism of the painting is unfavourable, suggesting duplicity.

Arousing emotions in a message and their reflectiveness can constitute relatively close forms of reception of an aesthetic work. Reflection as a purpose of a message is seen in a melancholy work by Hopper: *Office in a Small City*.

Here is a sunlit space with its organizing framework of bright building walls reflecting light. In the foreground, with two huge corner windows, but without panes, there is a building that seems to be a shell, an incomplete project. By a window, there is a very simple desk at which a man is sitting who stares above the roof of the opposite building, in the direction of implicit horizon. We see him in profile, dressed in a white shirt with rolled-up sleeves and a dark waistcoat. The 'office' he occupies stands in contrast to ornamentation of the opposite building. The view from the windows is open, but in the background, in the left of the composition, a massive dull wall seems to limit space, maybe symbolizing a kind of restriction. The delicate silhouette of the figure reveals the subtlety of the situation. The figure seems not to have a momentary break at work but to be deep in thought of an existential nature. Peace emanates from the painting.

Subtle reflection and an aura of mystery created by using the chiaroscuro technique are also characteristic of the photograph portraying the president of Lorillard Co., showing him standing, in three-quarter profile, with his hands in pockets or behind his back, which cannot be clearly seen because the figure is partly hidden in shadow.[3] He may face a window with its bright reflection seen on the office wall and creating a specific atmosphere of this photograph.[4]

The set of pictures that we interpreted also includes works with a favourable direction of communication, mainly photographs by Walker Evans forming the series Fortune Business Executive Profile. The portraits of Craig from AT&T show a likeable, slightly smiling man in a relaxed posture, looking confidently in the camera. Similarly, the portrait of McCollum from Continental Oil shows a broadly smiling, glad businessman, captured in sunlight, casually resting on a rail. The series of photographs *Portraits and Studies of Bankers at Work*, by the same author, portraying, for example, Joseph Barr, convey a picture of relaxed people in office space, in conversational situations. Viewing these works gives no impression of tension or stress. It can even be thought that they represent almost informal social occasions, if not for an obvious office environment in which the figures are portrayed. Finally, there is the work *Two Businessmen in Hats Talking on Street, Florida*, also by Evans, showing two gentlemen, with a rather jovial look, whose gestures, mimics, and postures make an impression of unrestrained confidence and evident satisfaction and bright smiles that easily infect the spectator.

Each work, be it text or painting, is created to carry a sense and results from the operationalization of the creative, artistic intent of its author. Most works interpreted by us, as shown in Chart 4.4, convey that sense in a correlational way (58.5%), which refers to representing figures captured in certain similarity between them – for example, in their clothes or positions. A significant set conveys sense in a contextual way (47.4%) – that is, linking the portrayed figure with history, social, political conditions or the physical environment. An example of correlational sense is provided by a majority of works by Evans, where figures not only are relatively formatted regarding their clothes but also seem to behave in front of the camera in a similar manner. If they sit in their office, they frequently adopt similar, relaxed, sometimes even casual positions. If they are portrayed during an activity, this is usually a telephone or face-to-face conversation, signing or browsing documents, necessarily with a fountain pen in hand.

The series of photographs indicated above show also the situational context by portraying figures in the office environment or during professional tasks. A work from the series *Portraits of M. J. Rathbone of Jersey Standard Oil* by Evans, showing in the right bottom a fragment of a figure sitting in a relaxed position with a cigarette in hand and presumably talking to the main figure in the photograph, presents an allusive context in which the spectator can guess whether the conversation is private or refers to a transaction or administrative affairs, or whether it is a casual visit from a friend.[5]

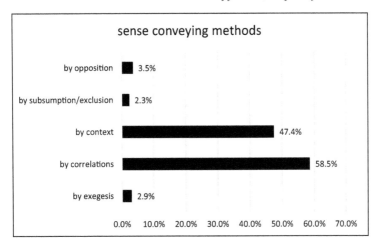

Chart 4.4 Structure of sense-conveying methods
Source: Authors own elaboration

The relaxed position of the interlocutor and a cigarette in his hand indicate certain cultural context characteristic of business relations in America of the 1950s.

A special example of contextual sense is also given in two works by Edward Hopper, *Office at Night* and *New York Office*, which by the positioning of figures relative to their surroundings and other participants create narratives, certainly depicting an office but extending far beyond a simple representation of office tasks. They thus invite the spectator to fill in the unspoken, continue the story told, and complement the tale in which the depicted theme, office, provides merely a background – context.

In the painting *Office at Night*, we see two figures: a receptionist standing at a filing cabinet and waiting for decisions by her boss, who sits behind a desk. These are two people in a hierarchic and professional relationship, portrayed in a manner perpetuating stereotypes about the division of occupational roles. But there is also another subtle interpretation layer: a woman and a man in a professional environment. The hour is late. The woman is depicted with emphasis on her physical attractiveness. She seems to wait not only for job instructions but also for attention from the man absorbed in documents and indifferent to his environment. When seeing the work, the following questions may arise: What does it actually depict? What deep interpretation layers are hidden in these layers of oil paint?

Other sense communication methods are also worth mentioning, even if they are represented by a small sample: namely, by opposition, exegesis, subsumption, and exclusion. They consist, respectively, of indicating concepts or images with opposite meanings, using contrast, showing the past importance of a figure, building, or interior, reminding of the importance of an object or individual, in a commendable or blameworthy sense, and representing a figure as the epitome of a social category, an example of a 'social type', being an integral part of a group or community (subsumption) or, contrarily, being insignificant for the event taking place, potentially excepted or marginalized (exclusion).

Examples of exegetic, in a sense, works can be seen in *Henry Crispe of the Custom House* by Thomas Frye or *The Cathedrals of Wall Street* by Florine Stettheimer. In the former work, the figure portrayed can be regarded as the personification of the importance and weight of the office he occupies. This is demonstrated by his posture, expensive clothes, richness, and splendour. Although this is not a past glory, because the figure depicted was then in office, it seems that by portraying him in this manner, the author implicitly reinforced the message about the meaning and importance of the institution represented by the portrayed.

The work by Stettheimer creates a completely different narrative dedicated explicitly to the 'splendour' of market institutions by depicting Wall Street, which with its banks and dominating building of the stock exchange sets a framework for modern social existence. However, the work refers, to an extent, to the glorious origins symbolized by the Statue of Liberty, personifying the values of the free world, even if the sculpture is placed in the distance and is not a dominant element of the painting.

The set of works that inspire our discussion has been selected in a uniform and coherent sampling process in which the main criterion was the occurrence of specific key words in titles; however, the set is relatively diverse, principally because it partly consists of paintings and graphics and partly of photographs that belong to a completely different communication medium. Photographs that certainly belong to the category of pictures aimed to capture a moment are distinct, for example, in means of expression – without texture, brushstrokes, and principally without drawing, traces of pencil that may significantly contribute to the understanding of the work's author intent. For this reason, paintings open a significantly larger space for interpretation and have a considerable potential for provoking various idiosyncrasies, unlike photographs that are rather uniform in their message, especially because most of them were taken by a single author whose artistic domain was to truthfully document reality. The indicated differences are illustrated by code clouds (Figures 4.1 and 4.2), which in the case of paintings reveal a distinct dominance of context as a sense transfer method and encourage reflection as a goal.

The cloud of codes referring to representations of business in paintings and graphics shown in Figure 4.1 indicates that this communication medium usually represents the context of a situation or figure, depicts figures in action, and aims at encouraging reflection. Groups are frequently portrayed, and the dominant direction of communication is neutral. People portrayed are more frequently active than passive.

Figure 4.1 Code cloud, paintings (min. frequency 5, 43 codes)

Source: Authors own elaboration

Figure 4.2 Code cloud, photographs (min. frequency 5, 49 codes)

Source: Authors own elaboration

Photographs, as shown in Figure 4.3, are characterized by exemplification – according to the author's artistic purpose, the figures photographed seem to be typical and are depicted as iconic representatives of a social group, a specific function, in equally typical, or even conventional, situations. They are more frequently passive than active, which means posed, captured in a moment of thought, reflection, looking in the camera, and much less frequently in a specific kind of action – for example, a conversation with another person. This type of message is also fact-oriented in its tone, relatively free of emotion – neutral. It does not seem that the author wished to leave in the photograph any mark of emotional involvement in the reality portrayed. The identified category of sense transfer by correlation refers to the fact that most figures portrayed wear similar clothes and are captured in similar situations and environment, resulting in considerable similarity between the objects depicted by the photographs.

The subject, goal, and direction of communication and sense transfer methods as the basic categories of content analysis are used to see a characteristic structure of aesthetic representations of the world of organizations. These depictions of individuals and groups show them in an emotionally neutral manner, as typical representatives, exemplifying their occupational group, profession, or social class. The representations also indicate a number of correlations, natural similarities, although the figures happen to be depicted in certain contexts. The figures are relaxed and remarkably confident.

The categories of figure characteristics and authority, added in open coding, and the category of values, coded using the typology of competing values (Maher, 2000) as well as individual and organizational values considered from the perspective of their congruence (Liedtka, 1989), are used to see a more nuanced picture of the organization and its people. The picture reveals a persona who is focused on their tasks, situation, interlocutor, or documents and confident.

4.1.2   The figure of boss – concentration and relaxed confidence

The distinguished figure characteristics, as shown in Table 4.1, include physical and personal traits. This semantic category is included in Berelson's content analysis and is complemented here by open coding.

We classify personality traits of a figure in groups: those displayed in the context of work done, occupational, and related to the situation and its managing by a person and relational, that is those describing the attitude towards others and surroundings. The dominant categories include, in this case, concentration, calmness, and confidence.

Confidence can be usually inferred from the posture, mimics, or gestures of the figures depicted. It is usually shown in a form of interaction with another person – for example, an interlocutor in the photograph, on the telephone,

Table 4.1 Selected figure characteristics (> 1% frequency)

Figure characteristics in communication	Frequency
Physical	
Repulsiveappearance	
Caricatured	1.2%
Ugliness	1.7%
Individualization	
Typological differentiation	1.5%
Dominating the scene	
Plumpness	1.5%
Ease	9.5%
Nonchalance	2.8%
Figure impersonality	
Anonymity	1.5%
Standardization	1.7%
Conventionalism	
Elegance	4.6%
Office wear	15.4%
Conventional wear	6.7%
Personality	
Working and professional	
Persistence, resolution	1.2%
Mindfulness	4.7%
Concentration	12.2%
Situational	
Provocative	1.1%
Calm, composure	4.9%
Relational	
Confidence	10.2%
Detachment	1.1%
Communicativeness	1.7%
Likeability	2.1%
Curiosity	2.6%

Source: Authors own elaboration

or the photographer doing the portrait. Be it a theatre manager calmly look-ing straight in the eyes from behind half-closed eyelids in the photograph by Sander (*Business Manager of a Theatre*) or a banker in a nonchalant and equally position sprawled in an armchair or sitting on a desk during a tel-ephone conversation or a discussion with another person in the photographs by Evans, or proudly erect, filling the entire picture frame figure of the 18th-century customs clerk with great ambitions and clear facial expression – the spectator gets the unmistakable feeling of internal strength and confidence emanating from the figure.

Figures are portrayed with various forms of concentration. They may focus on an interlocutor, as in the photographs by Evans, discussed in part earlier in this section, but most frequently they focus on documents. We see in such situations female office workers in *Untitled (Office Workers)*; officials or clerks in the 19th-century watercolour and gouache by Pieter de Josselin de Jong *In the office*; or businessmen in the egg tempera by Lawrence *(The Businessmen)*. In the last painting, documents seem to be a ubiquitous, key element in an otherwise reductionist composition. We see them in the form of papers spread on the floor, documents held in hand, or mysterious red folders, marking quite an interesting diagonal of the composition. They create a metaphor of a central problem, challenge, looked into, almost literally, by the figures united around a common cause.

The dominant traits of the figures are ease and confidence. They are depicted in conventional, mainly office, wear and focused on performing certain tasks or talking to others. The material subject to analysis also contains unfavourable representations of the world of organizations. For example, figures representing or even personifying business are caricatured or simply portrayed as ugly. We included these characteristics in a higher-level category of 'repulsive appearance', which is seen principally in abstractionist representations. An iconic example is the work by Condo, titled *Businessmen*, that was auctioned by Christie's.[6]

A similarly caricatured figure is seen in *Businesswoman* by Peter Saul, also an interesting example of individualization by her attire, provocatively inconsistent with the standard image of businesspeople. While understanding the satirical tone of that work and the irony that it emanates, we can propose its alternative interpretation: there is a person that wishes to emphasize her individuality and refuses to follow a convention. Perhaps today's businesspeople naturally moved away from standard clothes such as business suits or cocktail dress, and this type of convention is no longer binding, but in the late 1980s, when the work was created, that convention was rather generally observed. Thus, the picture of a person wearing sneakers and a green blouse that resembles something in between a jacket and a bathrobe may either ridicule and lampoon the figure portrayed as a stranger in the business community or emphasize the person's full autonomy from its control. Those negative physical traits are counterbalanced by representing business figures in a favourable light, as physically attractive individuals – simply handsome but principally emanating confidence and ease, which is seen in most photographs subject to analysis. The category of physical attractiveness of figures depicted may certainly be used in the context of works by Hopper, namely *Office at Night* and *New York Office*, which show a figure of an attractive woman in typical office environment.

However, seeing the graphics again, we must pay attention to a kind of impersonality in representing business objects – their form, frequently rather indefinite and dubious. The question arises whether they are humans or not, for example in the case of the painting by Maria Lassnig *Business Partners* – suggests full standardization – the figures are similar, have no distinguishing traits, represent a hazy form of being, with no room for diversity.

Consequently, they are characterized by anonymity. They are faceless exemplifications of a species.

Figure impersonality can also be expressed in a less abstract form, like in an etching by Carl M. Schultheiss from 1950 titled *Untitled (Office Workers)*, where the figures are as similar as to look like a series cast from the same mould, and their long-fingered, slender hands characteristically handling a typewriter or documents resemble those of manikins. They also fit in the category of conventionalism, characteristic of most works from that period, especially photographs, consisting principally of depicting standard office wear[7] and broadly understood clothes that follow a specific convention.

In works depicting organizations and the world of business, figures also occasionally appear who represent negative emotional states.[8] Sorrow, frustration, or depression are experienced by the figures depicted in the 1936 lithograph *Employment Office* by Gross-Bettelheim or in the linocut by Albert Potter *Organizational Advances* from the same period. However, neither work depicts business figures; they rather illustrate the consequences of organizational and economic processes, considering that the works represent the period of the Great Depression and show disadvantaged people who desperately take any job to survive, are completely unable to get a job, or are forced to register with an employment agency.

Figure characteristics and an assessment of authority and its sources are useful in complementing the initial structure of organizational representations and precisely indicating who is perceived as an epitome and personification of business.

4.1.3   An authority or keeper of information with proud and commanding sight

Authority is one of the key elements of the message content proposed by Berelson. The polysemy of this concept, which in its most general meaning refers to an entity – individual or institution – held in regard, having a great importance and gravity, for example, due to the office held, suggests multiple various sources of that regard. In other words, looking at a painting or a photograph, we ask the question, 'What is the reason for our perception of an individual as someone who is held in regard?' It was a code category complemented inductively in the open coding process. Several detailed associations that create an aura of authority about a portrayed figure are given in Table 4.4. They can be grouped to form higher-level categories. These include competence-based authority, which can be inferred from the fact that the portrayed figure is considering a decision to make, disciplining or supervising others, or explaining something. Another category is asset-based authority, where a major factor is knowledge or information possessed, which can be inferred from portraying the figure next to documents, records. The third category is authority inferred from the attitude towards others: the figure's posture or sight emanates domination, pride, confidence, and calm (Table 4.2).

Table 4.2 Authority and its sources

Authority	Frequency
Competence-based	
Making decision	8.5%
Instructing, disciplining	2.6%
Supervising	4.3%
Clarifying, explaining	12.8%
Asset-based	
Possessing information	15.4%
Attributes of power	6.0%
Based on attitude towards others	
Proud, dominating posture	24.8%
Calm, composure, confidence	7.7%
Proud/brave sight	17.9%

Source: Authors own elaboration

Importantly, research material shows no correlations of these traits and only contains illustrations of particular characteristics that constitute authority.

This interpretation is illustrated, for example, by multiple photographs of prominent figures, representatives of Chase, or the portrait of Henry Crispe. The latter figure fills the entire frame, which clearly symbolizes his domination over his surroundings, and the very posture and sight seem to speak for his feeling of power and agency. The photographs also reveal the importance of possessing information or access to information, which is symbolized by numerous documents spread on desks, frequently with an impressive size. This enables the figures depicted to take the role of someone clarifying and explaining things to others. The importance of documents, their central role as information sources, is also evident in such graphics as *Office Workers* or *Businessmen* by Lawrence, where they occupy a central place, catching the attention of the spectator and provoking the question about their contents that surely pose a challenge or problem for the people gathered around.

This points to the quite obvious conclusion that knowledge possessed, which is symbolized by various types of documents and records, allow to take a supervisory, dominating position over others who may be provided with information or not, or given its interpretation. This may take place in the spirit of partnership, consultation, as shown in the photographs where the 'boss', for example, leans on the desk in a casual posture, holding a conversation with a figure who is sitting or standing close.

4.1.4   *Values in business – success, relationships, and professionalism*

To determine the axiological message carried by paintings, we use the typology of competing values (Maher, 2000)[9] and organizational and individual values (Liedtka, 1989).[10] Table 4.3 contains those of them that occurred with relatively higher frequency in the analysed paintings and photographs.

Professionalism is a category inferred partly from the fact that the figure depicted follows certain conventions regarding image, with clothes as its quintessence, and partly from representations of specific office tasks performed by individuals with full attention and concentration, either on a conversation or on documents.

However, dominating themes in business paintings and photographs are success and achievements which may be represented by artefacts accompanying the figures portrayed, as in the case of photographs showing people from 3M – for example, its chief on the airstair of a private plane.[11]

However, in most cases success is only implied. Representations in paintings, and especially in photographs, provide little information about values, but the works usually portray individuals who could afford to commission a portrait by a prominent artist, like Sir Benjamin Truman, who was portrayed by Gainsborough, or people who by their professional history deserved to be featured in the *Fortune* magazine.

Values form the last category in this part of research, which is complemented by open coding and considered under a higher-level term of *focusing values*, such characteristics as professional orientation, future orientation, competitive struggle, and aggression (Table 4.3). These characteristics evidently emanate from some works, providing also certain value vectors that clearly communicate the nature of perception of the world of business by the work's author. Thus, professionalism may be attributed to the clerks depicted in the watercolour and gouache by Pieter Josselin de Jong (1861–1906) titled *In the Office*. Full concentration seen on the faces of the figures in the foreground and middle ground suggests priority for the work being done and an attitude free from any distraction. The fingers of the main figure's left hand, bony and taut, due to pressure on a sheet of paper, reflect the meticulousness and care taken to prevent any possible error.

Rigid white collar and impeccable tie indicate that everything in the work process must be in its proper place, which is typical of the bureaucratic vision of the world. In this sense, maybe even the bored trainee, still learning the profession, is also in his proper place, away from important tasks but close enough to observe how others perform their jobs.

The works also represent values that correspond to negative effects, but these are an inseparable element of each economic system, namely competitive struggle and its resultant – aggression. They seem to be accurately illustrated in the depressing work *Organizational Advances*, showing a crowd of chaotically moving individuals. Everyone moves here in a disorganized manner; they are presumably jostling and shoving to get a better location. They exemplify a crowd of alienated individuals. The fact that the work dates to the period of the Great Depression and its message: it depicts people advertising various businesses and products as a means to survive, graphically pressed in an existential framework between a fence with a garbage can behind it (the left

Table 4.3 Selected values (frequency >1%)

Values	Frequency
Focusing values	
Professional orientation	7.1%
Future orientation	1.4%
Competitive struggle	1.4%
Aggression	1.4%
Competing values	
Achievements	8.7%
Growth	2.8%
Profits	2.6%
Results	5.2%
Stability	2.8%
Formalization	2.4%
Discipline	3.3%
Security	2.1%
Control	2.4%
Interpersonal relationships	10.9%
Teamwork	1.4%
Cooperation	3.5%
Organizational versus individual values	
Money	2.8%
Success	14.9%
Expression of individuality	3.1%
Prestige	6.1%
Honesty	2.8%
Company reputation	1.4%

Source: Authors own elaboration

bottom of the composition) and a skyline of a modern city far on the horizon – justify the work's pessimistic mood. The figures seem to be located on the outskirts of an urban area, away from its rich and modern downtown – on the periphery, both in a literal and metaphoric sense, considering their hypothetical living conditions that may be indicated both from the work's expression and from the context of its creation. Competitive struggle may be personified here by figures packed together and fighting for their positions. The work can also be viewed in light of its title. Maybe it illustrates the competitive struggle between companies for the market for their products and services.

Attention is also drawn by what is missing or ignored in the message. This refers to values that are included in the analytical scheme we adopted but are not represented in any work to a degree allowing their coding. They include innovation, product quality, employee well-being, and leadership in an industry, all completely absent in research material, and productivity, continual improvement, adaptivity, creativity, entrepreneurship, centralization, helping others, life comfort, respect for others, customer service, integrity, organizational stability, value for community, utilitarianism, and tolerance of diversity and are represented to a negligible extent (below 1% code occurrence frequency).

While the characteristics of figures and the sources of their authority give a description of people of organizations, values should shed a brighter light on the environment that those people create. Combined with the primary structure of an aesthetic message – that is, the categories of goal and direction of communication and sense transfer methods – values inform how the world of organizations is commented, who personifies that world, and what is the platform for building relations between the world of organizations and its environment. The reductionist nature of value structure is evidenced by the significant predomination of few codes with a negligible importance of a large number of other codes that can be identified in aesthetic communications. This indicates that this is a world in which success and achievements dominate and form the principal axiological platform for organizational activity. The axiological aspect of this culture is limited. Interpersonal relationships are simplified in setting a framework of that activity – that is, by indicating that it is necessarily social and cannot be conducted in isolation, but the relations are not evaluated in terms of their good, generous, or bad qualitative context. No emergent categories appear that would refer to ethics or morale. Even the work with a subject explicitly concerning the giving of help and charitable causes (*Charity Organization Society*) creates in its message a narrative of social costs and benefits of aid, considering the historical and cultural contexts in which an assessment is made as to who deserves support or not, aimed to ensure that aid is not wasted.

4.2 Organizational tales

4.2.1 The space of emergent values

In the set of paintings and photographs, selected for analysis of organizational aesthetics, we identified the sphere of characteristics that was not directly given. The description we present results from a discussion on the meanings of identified characteristics and their dimensions that can be termed 'negotiating meaning' (Thomas et al., 2011; Lüscher & Lewis, 2008). That negotiation of meaning is not only a method of revealing latent, not readily visible characteristics of works, but also a method of intersubjective result control; like in participant observation where two observers can guarantee a better reliability of observation results, in our study two researchers mutually controlled their perception of events, situations, and figures depicted in the selected works. The procedure resulted in indicating the dimensions[12] in which to consider the individuals, situations, and events from the world of organizations portrayed by artists.

The 11 codes defined inductively by aggregating more detailed description categories of works actually correspond to the parameters of the organizational or corporate reality as perceived by artists and their perception of human types, events, and situations depicted in paintings or captured in photographs. The presented lists of attributes that we identified in the works analysed locate the phenomena of organizational world in a highly diverse sphere of characteristics. The principal dimensions illustrate the 'themes' that attract the attention of artists. Table 4.4 shows that most attributes refer to figure characteristics, stereotypes and conventions, depicted phenomena, environment, and relationships. Only few refer to time and community.

The emphasis on figure characteristics results to a considerable extent from the 'corpus' of material selected by us for analysis. Their major part consisted of photographs depicting prominent business figures; also, the paintings represented such figures from more remote periods.

In material subject to analysis, three categories are distinguished in the code 'figure characteristics': official, player, and homo liber.

The official belongs to the sphere of administration, performs tasks assigned by his supervisor, local or central authorities. Officials are portrayed by 18th- and 19th-century painters in typical period clothes, rooms, and with characteristic artefacts – for example, holding a quill in hand. The role of official is characterized by stability, meticulousness, and concentration. The category of 'official' is further developed by four secondary indicators: performing the role (i.e. completing tasks in an office), indifference (not necessarily as a sign of disregard for the client, also as the absence of emotions, unemotionality), meticulousness (immersion in work, focus on task, visible in the figure leaning over the desk, documents, with sight focused on fields completed), standardization (conventionalism, copying the pattern of representing an official, emphasis on the characteristics indicated above in the portrait).

Another figure is a player. Someone who goes beyond the corporate and organizational boundaries, is resistant to standardization, does not fit established

Table 4.4 Frequency of primary categories in paintings and photographs

Codes	Photographs	Paintings
Attributes of management	3.9%	9.6%
Relationships	7.8%	6.8%
Stereotypes and conventions	15.9%	7.3%
Approach to tasks	3.6%	4.1%
Perception	11.4%	0.9%
Time	2.1%	1.8%
Environment	5.1%	13.2%
Space	0	11.0%
Community	0.6%	8.2%
Business figures	42.6%	24.7%
Illustration of a phenomenon	6.9%	12.3%

Source: Authors own elaboration

frameworks. This is seen in a series of secondary labels – demonstrated frustration, depression, reflection (thought), reserve, but also adaptation to the circumstances, showing the diversity of figures. The player has also other secondary characteristics: eccentricity, astuteness, duplicity (showing a face of Janus), confidence, doggedness, haughtiness, cunning, position of power, determination, avarice, thoughtlessness.

The third 'view' is homo liber or a free individual[13] – someone who frequently is plump, has an attractive appearance, is calm, shows a cheerful disposition, and is elegant, relaxed, and more specifically nonchalant, demonstrating this attitude by casual positions, for example sprawled in an armchair, but also a hedonist.[14]

The great importance of the 'stereotypes and conventions' dimension results principally from its connection with the first category – business figures. The figures in paintings and photographs are quite frequently portrayed as illustrations of certain stereotypes of people from the world of organizations.

The phenomenon and environment are two additional main categories. The relatively high frequency of their occurrence is explained by the fact that they describe the context in which the figures appear. In a narrower perspective this is a phenomenon, and in a wider perspective, the environment. However, sometimes the artist's interest is focused on a phenomenon or environment as such to the exclusion of portraying a figure.

The code termed 'perception' again refers to the figure. We interpret this category based on a reaction to what is seen by the individual or individuals portrayed. We distinguish two primary indicators: non-oriented perception (sight is not directed to a person or situation and reveals no interest of the subject in something or someone in the environment) and oriented perception (sight is clearly directed to someone or something, indicates concentration, mindfulness).

Attributes of management infrequently appear in the works and usually emphasize the importance of figure, suggesting hard work or contact with the external world as a domain of individuals occupying supervisory positions. This category does not seem to be complex. It occurs in the analysed works only in the form of primary indicators, as a sign of contact with the external world (telephone), as a 'walking staff' illustrating the life of an organization member as a travelling person who also needs aid or support, as a fountain pen used to record or write. Finally, the set of attributes includes folders, records, and documents held in hands or put on desks of the individuals portrayed.

Portraits form a significant part of our research material. Background is treated as an addition to the portrait of an individual, or is reduced to a margin of little significance. The category of approach to tasks includes a continuum ranging from hierarchical work organization and bureaucracy to chaos, with neutrally depicted job-performance activities falling 'in between'.

We were seldom given the possibility of applying the category of time to the events and individuals represented. The importance of time is accentuated by artists giving titles to selected paintings and photographs, such as *Young Businessman*, or representing middle-aged or old people. Associations with time are evoked by artefacts seen in some works, such as a clock or calendar.

The dialogue phase is aimed at identifying and negotiating key associations evoked by pictures of business figures and of the world of organizations. In the process of defining primary categories, by way of aggregating basic emergent codes with a view on their similarity, attention is attracted to differences in saturation with codes between paintings and graphic material (Table 4.4). The category of codes with the largest representation includes those defining *figure characteristics* (35.5%), then *stereotypes and conventions* (12.5%), in both cases being most explicit in the photographs.

In the material collected, stereotypes can principally be reduced to representing the roles of men and women in the world of organizations and management – that is, showing the agency of men and the menial and the subordinate or ancillary role of women. Conventions refer only to conventional wear outside office and formal wear in the office. Conventionalism of clothes in more recent times – in photographs – confirms a developed 'dress code' applicable in organizations.

Stereotypes and conventions refer to clothes, usually characteristic of a social class, as in the case of a painting by Degas, *Portraits at the Stock Exchange*, or the 1937 photograph depicting a similar community, *London Stock Exchange, a Typical Young Businessman*, by Emil Otto Hoppe.

The first work depicts a group of three gentlemen. They fully deserve this term, due to their distinguished appearance and elegant clothes. All of them wear top hats. The central figure makes the impression of a respectable man with a wealth of life experience, a source of his calm wisdom of a player who is not a newcomer. This impression is reinforced by the cane he leans on, and his oval face with sharpened features behind glasses.[15] Obviously, the figures depicted in the sketch belong to the same social group and are connected by cultural links. This affiliation to a certain kind of caste becomes more explicit in an oil version of the work,[16] where the colour scheme is more uniform, and the main group is surrounded by other participants in the event whose features are unrecognizable – they are only suggested by colour areas without clear drawing that would more clearly define form contour, but we recognize their presence and identity shared with the protagonists by the symbolism of clothes. It could be concluded that such clothes were characteristic of the period; that was the 'fashion' of the time. However, not everyone wore such clothes; they were reserved for a social stratum, – for example, stock traders and investors. The aesthetic resemblance between the painting by Degas and the photograph *London Stock Exchange, a Typical Young Businessman* is obvious, although the two representations are distant in time and space. The portrait at the Paris Stock Exchange was created in the 1870s and the photograph at the London Stock Exchange, or more precisely in front of its building – probably in the 20th century.[17]

The figure of a young businessman with a supremely elegant appearance, in a dark jacket with a vest, a tie, trousers from fine material, and wearing his top hat as naturally as others wear their more common head coverings, is indicative of his membership in the same social group as that of the Parisian traders.

Business, office wear, characteristic of the managerial staff, can be observed in almost all photographs taken by Walker Evans or in the emblematic portrait of Max Roesberg by Otto Dix, where the figure's clothes are quite a uniform – an iconic symbol of working in business. The last work is free from ostentation and chic, so explicit in the two former works. The figure is depicted in clothes that can be described as formal rather than elegant. He is still a man of business and trading but viewed mainly as a man of labour.

The third most represented concept category is *illustration of a phenomenon* (9.1%), wherein depictions in paintings are more representative.

In our reception, visual representations of business illustrate prestige in the first place, then secrecy and contrast and duplicity, as shown in Chart 4.5.

Prestige builds barriers or is identical with barriers. Not everyone can enter the offices of executives or the organization building. Some interactions may be reserved for a select group – for example, trusted consultants, shareholders, colleagues, employees or business partners. Easy access, the absence of social boundaries between classes or groups would make the world of organizations inclusive and open to all who wish to enter that world. We are perfectly aware that organizations cannot be inclusive in this sense – they may not accept just anybody, especially in positions that require competence, knowledge and

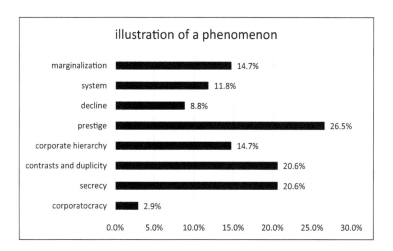

Chart 4.5 Structure of codes illustrating phenomenon

Source: Authors own elaboration

skills. The prestige associated with the brand of organization one works for, with the role performed or position held, related to socioeconomic status, makes an organization an object of aspirations. Prestige protects from undesirable inclusiveness, creates a barrier and frame of reference for potential followers. It is a powerful motivator, mainly in individualistic cultures, as researchers argue (Bellah, 1985). Thus, we have directors or chief executives sitting at their desks in positions not infrequently revealing a quite nonchalant attitude, on the one hand, and people listening, waiting, or performing tasks assigned by supervisors, on the other hand.

The differences between photographs, and paintings and graphics, in the context of representing certain phenomena are illustrated in Table 4.5.

Prestige has to be visualized and is more frequently depicted in photographs than in paintings. For example, the president of 3M is portrayed with a plane in the background, presumably a private or corporate aircraft. Prestige is indicated by attributes of power, such as huge desks at which bankers sit. Imagine an office room with its walls lined using fine panels, maybe wainscoting, in a bright colour. There is an arched entrance to another room in the background. At one side, next to the wall, there is a sofa for guests that is upholstered in leather or satin, which is also used to finish an armchair with elegantly curved armrests. The central part of the photograph is occupied by a desk of an impressive size, with a top shining like a piano lid, reflecting light from side lamps installed on the wall on both sides of the arched door frame. A man sits at the desk on which documents are arranged quite symmetrically. He seems to be one of the many elements of interior design in this office room. The size of his figure compared to the other objects depicted in the photograph, especially the desk, indicates that these surrounding objects are equally important as the man at the desk. They have to create an adequate space for his actions: they symbolize his powers. They reflect those powers.

The series of photographs by Walker Evans portraying bankers at work, the backgrounds, and the surroundings of the figures portrayed show that they

Table 4.5 Phenomena in paintings and photographs

Illustration of a phenomenon	*Photographs*	*Paintings*
Corporatocracy	0	11.1%
Secrecy	13.0%	18.5%
Contrasts and duplicity	4.3%	25.9%
Corporate hierarchy	17.4%	3.7%
Prestige	52.2%	3.7%
Decline	4.3%	7.4%
System	0	18.5%
Marginalization	8.7%	11.1%

Source: Authors own elaboration

are affluent people with considerable achievements who are 'on home turf' in the world they have created.

The dominant phenomenon illustrated in graphics is contrasts and system, as seen not only in abstractionist works but also in those by Nevinson. The pastel work titled *From an Office Window*[18] by this artist depicts an urban landscape with an industrial character. It consists of geometric forms that represent outlines of buildings. The space is intersected by power lines that may also suggest the layout of streets, invisible from above. The verticals of buildings, the horizontals and slants of power lines, suggesting recession and perspective, jointly create the impression of a schematic layout – a system of interconnected elements. Its mechanical character is reinforced by a very limited colour scheme – all objects are represented in shades of grey, between the black window frame and white light or smoke over building roofs. The impression of cold and certain inhumanity of this environment is strengthened by few accents in cool blue. However, this is not the sky which is absent in this work but rather reflections of light in window panes.

The organizational or corporate hierarchy also belongs to phenomena. The aim is not to give a dynamic picture of the organization but rather a snapshot depicting momentum. Structure is what seems to be a relatively durable element of reality. Process refers to organizational dynamics, to change. A structure exists, a process takes place or 'goes on'. In our opinion, both concepts will be necessary: structure may not be ignored to focus solely on processes. Structure and process are not alternatives but complementary phenomena explaining each other. We have to do with a portrait of organizational hierarchy when a work depicts two figures, one sitting behind and the other in front of a desk.[19] This can be an employee or client, rather not a business partner. The situation is clearly structured – the figure in front of the desk is from the outside, or from a lower level in the hierarchy. Hierarchy is also a sign of balance, of preventing entropy. Entropy is the negation of order, while hierarchy is an enormously strong indicator of order, although surely not always desirable.

The fourth most frequent coding category of *environment* is represented mainly in paintings and graphics which are probably connected to the fact that paintings build sense through a context with the environment as its key element.

The category of environment reveals the greatest number of constituents in the works analysed. It is a set of configurations captured by the artist and showing parts of the context of actions taken by the individuals portrayed, that is, including other people, institutions, material artefacts (buildings or edifices), symbols (names of institutions, portraits of important persons). Three main meanings of 'environment' are distinguished. It appears as a situational framework, complemented by two secondary indicators, that is surroundings with its depressing quality underlined by grey-shade colours and the absence of lively colour accents – limiting, binding its participants. It can take the form of an existential framework, pushing people into certain circumstances, actual or symbolic, determining their living options in a long time (existentially). Finally, the environment provides responses. It can be perceived as a set of chances, threats, as oppressive or encouraging.

The structure and frequency of the conceptual category of environment shown in Chart 4.6 suggest that the environment can build situational frameworks that we define from a short-term perspective or existential frameworks if it sets long-term conditions. We classify in the first category an environment that is depressing and creates various forms of oppression – for example, an environment that gives the feeling of being trapped.

Reaction to the environment, the widest category in the code structure (85.7%) as shown in Chart 4.6, took the form of integration with the environment, understood as belonging to a place or a class of people, surrender, or distance: signals of limited openness to others, seen in 'body language' and the position of hands. This code category also includes the approach to risk, complemented by secondary codes, such as conservatism, that is demonstrating caution, hesitation, uncertainty, seen in the position of the subjects portrayed, seeking support, balance, that is aiming at a central position and avoiding extremities, and risk-taking understood as behaviours close to that of self-preservation – for example, taking a position posing the danger of falling.

Depictions of the world of organizations, as is shown in Chart 4.7, frequently reveal a tendency to distancing from the environment and its other participants.

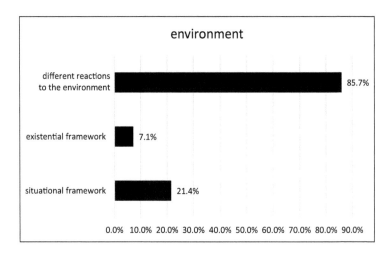

Chart 4.6 Structure of codes relating to environment

Source: Authors own elaboration

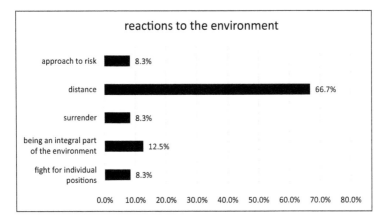

Chart 4.7 Different reactions to environment

Source: Authors own elaboration

We feel distance when looking at the work by the New York artist Edward Hopper (1882–1967) *Office in a Small City* from 1953.[20] In the bright space of the painting, with its dominant colours of blue sky and sunlit bright building walls, there is a man sitting who wears modest office clothes. He is sitting at a minimalist desk and gazing outside.

He seems to be deep in unrestrained thought. There are no direct barriers, and the windows are free of frames and panes – being only outlined in the office walls and providing enormously wide openings to the outside world. This seems to allow free far-reaching sight up to the horizon that is not explicitly shown but presumed in the line of sight of the figure depicted. We guess that the man wants to live without limitations. He would be happy to escape from his environment; basically, there is nothing to hold him. Maybe this is a man making a decision to leave, saying in his mind goodbye to his existing environment. And maybe he is someone kept by invisible ties. The figure looking at the far distance is thrown into a muse. He personifies loneliness of someone who has a high position or high hopes, or escapes from reality into distant dreams.

Distance can also be manifested in a less metaphorical way, using body language, little gestures, and postures in specific situations – for example, by hands in pockets, revealing a secretive attitude, caution in interaction with others. This impression can be formed when looking at a figure with casual posture standing against a wall – with relaxed arms, both hands in pockets, the left foot put slightly forward, the left arm seeming to slightly lean against the wall.

The arms folded across the chest show distance to the speaker. Imagine an elegant office with discrete light from a side lamp and a portrait on the wall, showing presumably the company's founder. The portrait forms the background for a desk with a businessman leaning against it, in a loose suit, with his arms folded across the chest, and his hands under his forearms. He talks to someone – listens to a thoughtful figure in front of him. His head is directed slightly to the side, he does not listen to the interlocutor with full attention.[21] His mind occupied by other matters makes him detached from the conversation, maybe one of those repeatedly held each and every day.

Distance from the environment and the specific situation is also displayed by the young lady in a green dress, in the right top of *Charity Organization Society*.[22] The central part of the scene is occupied by a bulky figure of a plump individual sprawled casually in a chair and wagging his finger at a shy, slim man with his head humbly hung, standing to the left in front of a body of those evaluating him. This applicant is seeking aid from philanthropists before a judge who decides whether or not assistance is to be provided. Behind the figure of the judge, there is a group of emotional people – their attitude towards the applicant is rather unfavourable. Their mimics seem to indicate their affinity in beliefs and perspective with those represented by the judge. The lady in green to the right even shows a sign of irritation. The smile on her face is sympathetic, but her body is partly turned away from the scene, and the nonchalant hand gesture seems to suggest that she is there by accident. Her slightly nonchalant posture stands in clear contrast with those of the emotionally engaged central group of figures. She seems to remain in her own world and be indifferent to the judgement made by the respectable body of philanthropists who are to decide whether the applicant for aid deserves support. She distances herself from the result of their proceedings: maybe it is distance from those in need or to human poverty that presumably does not affect that lady?

Reaction to the environment also includes the attitude towards the risks that it may pose, an attitude that we describe as conservatism, keeping balance and risk-taking, These three attitudes are brilliantly illustrated in the 1998 work *Geschaeftspartner (Business Partners)*, painted by the German artist Maria Lassnig (born 1919).[23] Imagine an amaranth background free of any detail with a kind of tree branch emerging – thin, growing off an equally thin trunk. Three figures are sitting on the branch. They seem to display certain traits of human form but are outlined only fragmentarily, as rough silhouettes, suggestively but without details. These sketchy forms are with potbellies, without hands or arms, without facial features, except one eye of the central individual. The figure next to the trunk, with presumably safe backing, fights for not being detached from that support. The central figure is exposed to external forces and seeks balance between them to survive. The figure is unsupported, weaving, looking for an equilibrium. And maybe this position is a metaphor of 'betting on multiple horses in a race' and symbolizes a comfortable centre? The posture and location of a figure in the composition (all are sitting on an overloaded branch) show the risk appetite of the players. The individual strongly attached to support behind his back emanates the will to retain security. Taking a position in between extremities indicates a moderate risk. Interestingly, the central figure is the only one to have an eye and thus is capable of seeing things. This can be man of the moment for the group, the only one who sees and can both encourage cowards and curb risk-takers – the only one who sees the circumstances, threats, and opportunities. Finally, to the right of the composition, there is a figure representing the attitude of bravery, irresponsibility. A figure dangerously situated on the edge of support who may fall or cause the foundation supporting the others to break. This attitude exposes others to hazard, means ignorance of potential consequences and risk. His potbelly that can be a caricature symbol of greed and avarice may throw off balance the figure that seems to be on the edge of fall, facing an imminent disaster.

A wider view on the work of Lassnig leads to reflection that certain figures in her paintings seem to personify a kind of madness. Obviously, they experience strong emotions, are absorbed in their internal world although incapable of describing and verbalizing it, because they are affected by a mysterious communicative impotence. Sometimes they have a single eye looking in an indefinite direction, or have no mouth. They happen to be unrooted in their environment, seem to float in the painting space characterized by sparseness in background and detail. Lassnig described her work as 'body awareness painting', which should be understood as painting from nature. In this context, *Business Partners* appear to be paradoxically represented in a dehumanized form, although resembling in their contour some humanoid silhouettes.

Saturation of paintings and graphics compared to photographs with the aspects of environment varies, as shown in Table 4.6.

Table 4.6 Representations of the environment theme in photographs and paintings (coding frequency)

Environment	Photographs	Paintings
Situational framework	0	17.2%
Depressing environment	0	10.3%
Confinement	5.9%	6.9%
Existential framework	0	10.3%
Fight for individual positions	0	6.9%
Being an integral part of the environment	5.9%	6.9%
Surrender	0	6.9%
Distance	88.2%	6.9%
Approach to risk	0	3.4%
Conservatism	0	17.2%
Balance	0	3.4%
Risk-taking	0	3.4%

Source: Authors own elaboration

The photographs represent distance, while paintings – situational frame-works and conservatism. The analysed photographs focus on interpreting the characteristics of the environment, which in the paintings under study can function as both a background and a space of symbols and more or less explicit meanings – thus, evocative and expressive framing can appear in paintings, as in the case of works by Stettheimer or Bettelheim. The role of framing, which is also used to organize the painting space as its centre of gravity with other elements of the composition located relative to that centre, is performed in the work by Stettheimer by the geometric, classical-style form of stock exchange building set between horizontal, geometric blocks of bank buildings to the left and vertical columns of the building to the right. In the work by Bettel-heim, the focal object is the diagonal counter, with the unemployed leaning on it at the *Employment Office*; the counter also marks spatial recession in the composition, suggesting the hierarchy of figures, further confirmed in their essentially linear representation where the line of arm of one figure overlaps another figure, thus marking the picture's foreground and middle ground.

The photographic works mainly depict figures, and the background is equally standard and secondary in its meaning.

Emergent codes also include space. This category is more general than the 'environment' as it refers to the place where something is located or goes on. Environment is situated in a geographic, social, or cultural space.

The works subject to analysis depict space in four primary dimensions. We distinguish the dimension of limited resources, represented as economical management and use and further developed by two secondary dimensions: minimalism and figures packed together – the dimension of an imposed for-mat, configuration, spatial order, and the dimensions of spatial hierarchy and organizational depth. Spatial hierarchy is further developed by three second-ary dimensions. They include the foundation of the organization, segmenta-tion, and dominant structure. Regarding the foundation, an artwork basically addresses the topic of ontology of the organization and answers the question as to how the organization exists. The foundation means roots, embedded-ness, or basis supporting the entire structure of a company or organization. An imposed spatial format may seem identical with a spatial hierarchy, but formatting has a wider sense. It refers to aspects dictated by the requirements of the task completion process, such as the arrangement of desks or worksta-tions in an office room or on a shop floor. From the 'segmenting' perspective, the space of organizations is divided into spheres managed by various people and businesses, specialists, occupiers of various roles. Segmentation may oc-casionally result from space formatting dictated by the logic of work pro-cesses, for example, separating various places for tasks to be performed. The dominant structure is a secondary category in a hierarchically defined space; it refers to differentiating the sizes of figures and material objects represented in a work and the presence of large buildings and tiny humans 'overshadowed' by those structures. Finally, the organizational depth refers to visualization of the organization and its context as a 'three-dimensional solid' rather than a 'plane' and allows using perspective with its foreground and middle ground.

Space is a natural element of a painting, as shown in Table 4.4. Space is organized predominantly in an economical way, like in *Office Workers*,[24] where this results in figures being packed together, evoking associations with a shop floor, or in today's language, with a call centre in which everyone has a strictly defined work area in a truly geometric style.

The way of space representation in a work also symbolically indicates a hierarchy that makes certain elements more important than others. A spatial hierarchy can take the form of a minimalist style in arranging the environment which may suggest opening, metaphorically, free space for creativity and activity. In this sense, a symbolic illustration is given in the sketch design of an office by André Arbus[25] depicting a cold, elegant interior. Sight is first directed to a structure looking like a room divider or screen, something used to arrange separate areas in an otherwise open space, considering the drawing's composition. However, as we continue to look at the picture, that dominant structure seems to take on weight, submit to gravity, to be set more firmly than could appear at the first sight. Subtle graphic elements seen on it suggest that this is a wall that can be treated metaphorically as a dominant structure, abstract in its form. The central position of the desk suggests a high rank of the person who will take a seat behind it; however, interestingly, a simple work chair is placed there. The elegant armchair for a visitor suggests that this can be a partner in conversation rather than an applicant, but although that interlocutor will take a comfortable position in the armchair, still it will be a lower position in terms of authority and hierarchy, as indicated by the line of the desktop situated considerably above the space intended for the interlocutor. There is no other armchair which may suggest that conversation will be held 'from behind the desk', creating a symbolic relation of power and hierarchy. However, the person to sit behind the desk and take that dominant position will be at work and not in a comfortable situation – this is indicated by the chair with a rather Spartan look. Attention is attracted to the solid structural component supporting the desk, but also a human figure at the base, an ornament, supporting the top with its head. Considering this not only in aesthetic but also symbolic terms, it can be argued that we are given an indication of the key role of people, their intellectual capital as a foundation of the organization. The space is designed in a minimalist style, drawn in cool colour tones and suggesting that there is no place for emotions.

The paintings are also the main area of depicting a community (Chart 4.8), where the dominant category of team (41.7%), is followed by the category of influential actors (33.3%) who can be figures of public life and finance, like in the Stettheimer's work, or not precisely identified members of a less honourable community of the underworld or mob, like in the 1992 work by Jason Rhoades with an intriguing title *Business as Usual*.[26] The latter work is a collage composed of photographs, depicting figures in suits absorbed in a

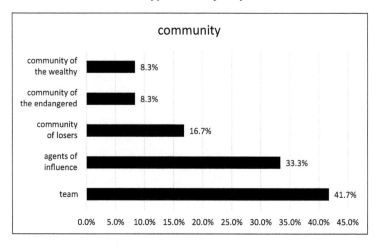

Chart 4.8 Structure of community depictions

Source: Authors own elaboration

confidential conversation, sitting behind a table with documents or standing at a car from the Prohibition era, next to a ramp, in a backyard of a building that looks like a warehouse. There is also a gathering, presumably political, in a session hall, a stylish theatre auditorium packed with the audience, and a political demonstration. Pacifist slogans are inserted in between the photographs. While the painting titled *The Cathedrals of Wall Street*[27] by Stettheimer seems to illustrate interrelations between influential actors from the world of politics and business in an elegant way, even celebrating a social system without showing clear disapproval of that system, the collage by Rhoades is an illustration with a distinct ethical quality. The work indicates that everything can be used to make profit regardless of circumstances, and things remain the same, nothing changes despite experience gained by the human race throughout history. Considering the meaning of the idiomatic expression 'business as usual', this interpretation is reasonable. The figures in the photographs are influential actors, people of business and politics whose interrelations are illustrated by the author without paying much attention to political correctness of his message.

The concept of relationship refers to interpersonal relationships and the way of their representation in selected works. This category includes primary indicators distinguishing between domination, indifference, and cooperation, according to the representation of coding frequency in Chart 4.9. The category of 'domination' was identified on the basis of such indicators as upright posture, standing position, looking straight ahead, in the interlocutor's eyes.

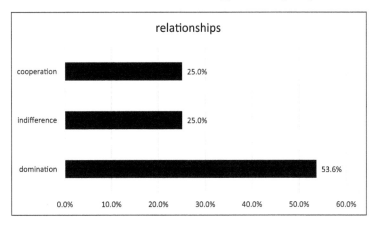

Chart 4.9 Relationships structure

Source: Authors own elaboration

The category of 'cooperation' is defined by conversation, action directed towards partner, responding to someone else's behaviour, reciprocity. The category of 'indifference' had to be defined using secondary codes – that is, the absence of interest and social bonds and alienation demonstrated in a work. The reason is that 'indifference' is not as unambiguous as domination or cooperation. Indifference may be depicted as the absence of interaction between individual, as marginalization of figures, for example, located in the middle ground, in a corner; lack of interest and boredom, or finally as alienation – that is, such arrangement of the physical work environment that prevents free interaction. Regarding frequency, the code category defining business relationships refers mainly to domination.

Dominance is characteristic of the figure of Henry Crispe[28] as depicted in the 1746 portrait by Thomas Frye (1710–1762). We see an impressive, plump individual with fleshy red lips, wearing enormously expensive clothes, with a proud look of a man who is satisfied with his life. He gently holds a quill in his plump, well-manicured hand.

The painting clearly reveals the artist's fascination with the play of light and admiration for the man portrayed and mainly emphasizes his status as a public figure. The painting shows writing materials, reflecting his poetic and literary ambition and talent that were desirable along with political skills in every man of business at that time (Gallery label, August 2004, www.tate. org.uk/art/artworks/frye-henry-crispe-of-the-custom-house-t05784, accessed: 3.08.23).

An illustration of domination is given in the photographs showing a businessman from Southern Pacific. The figure, although wearing clothes different from those seen in the portrait of Henry Crispe and characteristic of another period, an unassuming trench coat and a wide-brimmed hat, shows a certain similarity with the previously discussed example. Also, here we see some plumpness in the bulky man wearing the coat and his double chin. Portraying an individual in an unidentified place, but obviously on a tall building with a view on city panorama, at a height that requires safety grid installed, can also be interpreted as a symbol of domination of the represented institution over its environment. Finally, the *Travelling businessman, Rhineland* from 1930,[29] portrayed by August Sander, displays similar physical characteristics: a plump man with a bulky figure; he is captured in a rather unattractive setting, next to a shabby wall, presumably in a small town in the provinces, but still makes an impression of someone who knows his purpose, steps boldly, dominating the space with his persona.

Table 4.7 illustrates differences in saturation of photographs and paintings with various categories of relationship.

Domination and cooperation are the themes addressed in photographs, while indifference or even alienation is expressed in graphics and paintings. Domination is characterized not only by posture but also by a figure filling the entire frame or its major part. The indifference shown in paintings may take various forms, but usually it is visible as the absence of interaction, eye contact with other figures, like in Hopper's works *Office at Night*[30] and *New York Office*,[31] or in *Office Workers* and *Organizational Advances*, where everyone is focused on themselves.

It is worth mentioning that representations of business figures are frequently accompanied by artefacts, objects considered to be more or less characteristic of the positions occupied or tasks performed. Most representations show papers and documents, in the form of folders in the painting *Businessmen* by Jacob Lawrence,[32] a mysterious letter in Hopper's *New York Office*, a system of drawers in a filing cabinet in *Office at Night*), also by Hopper, or piles of documents on executives' desks in the photographs taken by Evans. However, people of the world of organizations happen to be portrayed with 'non-intuitive' accessories. Attention is surely drawn here to the walking staff

Table 4.7 Saturation of photographs and paintings with various categories of relationships

Relationships	Photographs	Paintings
Domination	65.4%	6.7%
Indifference	0	40.0%
Lack of interest	0	13.3%
Alienation	0	26.7%
Lack of bonds	0	13.3%
Cooperation	34.6%	0

Source: Authors own elaboration

or stick held by Sir Benjamin Truman in *Travelling Businessman* or by Ernest May portrayed by Edward Degas at the Paris Stock Exchange.

Thematic categories identified in the dialogue process and worth mentioning, although they are relatively insignificant as measured by their frequency in coded material, include the approach to tasks and time.

The category of approach to tasks, or in other words, the attitude towards tasks as illustrated by a painter or photographer and translated into primary codes, is defined as a metaphorical or symbolic expression of an attitude, waiting for decisions, a chaotic approach illustrating business 'polyphony' and underlined by the clothes worn by a figure or a caricatured combination of the figure's elements, hierarchical work organization and bureaucracy, and consultations.

The diversity of analytic material in this respect is shown in Table 4.8.

Waiting for decisions and consultations are depicted in photographs that frequently show their subject in conversation with another person, while paintings show complex work-related situations, such as the hierarchical order seen in the works by de Jong or Hopper, or chaos seen in the lampooning work by Peter Saul, or the problem-solving process evident in the work by Lawrence.

We see an interesting aspect of the dynamics of the emergent categories in their potential interrelations measured by the frequency of their co-existence. Chart 4.10 shows two such interrelations. In a considerable number of cases (80%), distancing from the environment occurred together with a consultative approach to tasks. This can be interpreted in terms of seeking opinion and confronting one's beliefs with the judgement of others without necessarily identifying with alternative points of view. In the context of business plans, a consultation is surely held to gather multiple points of view and assess them critically as a useful contribution to personal decision-making. Distance is thus natural in that context.

There is also an interesting correlation between chaos as an approach to performing tasks and a fight for individual positions in reaction to environmental conditions. Also in this case, the correlation is rather intuitive, assuming that cooperation requires that organizational entropy be reduced,

Table 4.8 Approaches to tasks as portrayed in photographs and paintings

Approach to tasks	Photographs	Paintings
Solving a problem	0	22.2%
Waiting for decisions	41.7%	11.1%
Chaos	0	22.2%
Hierarchical work organization and bureaucracy	0	44.4%
Consultations	58.3%	0

Source: Authors own elaboration

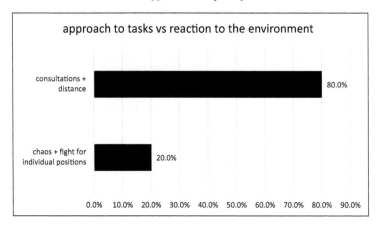

Chart 4.10 Interrelations of emergent categories

Source: Authors own elaboration

while chaos – that is, the absence of organized or even hierarchical forms of cooperation – promotes competitive struggle without providing motivation in the form of a specific common goal.

Reflection on the atmosphere of business representations, both in paintings and in photographs, reveals a subtle veil of time surrounding the figures or situations portrayed, as shown in Table 4.9. Certain nostalgic feelings appear there, which we perceive as past orientation (the codes *passing time* and *memory of the past*), as well as projecting oneself into the future, related explicitly with plans or another form of seeking future opportunities (the codes *window on the world* and *longing for the next step*).

Time, an inseparable component of the context in which people of organizations act, a measure of progress, of a perspective adopted, memory of things past, is visible in the analysed artistic works in its four facets (Chart 4.11).

First, time as a 'window on the world', future prospects, the horizon of individual or business opportunities. Second, time as a shrinking resource, passing time, signalled by such accessories as a clock or calendar. Third, time as the longing for another step, seen in portraying young entrepreneurs or businessmen. Fourth, time as the remembered, 'better' past, free from so many traps, threats and complications, a reflection of mythical thinking about the times of happiness, peace, glory, accentuated by portraits of prominent predecessors, founders of the corporation – pictures hung on the walls of the depicted offices.

The representations discussed mostly show various forms of memory of the past.

Here is a photograph representing a slightly embarrassed manager in a small office room in Butte, Montana.[33]

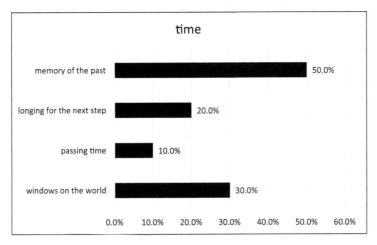

Chart 4.11 Meaning of time

Source: Authors own elaboration

Butte is a small town known as a centre of surface mining and mining machinery engineering. The photograph dates back to 1956. The time of taking the photograph was crucial for further history of that town with a population of 30,000. In the 1950s, in view of fierce competition, growing costs, and risks in underground mining, the Anaconda Co. corporation decided to invest in surface mines. In 1954, the corporation bought and demolished thousands of houses in the area to open a surface copper mine, Berkeley Pit (www.intermountainhistories.org/items/show/376, accessed: 28.08.2023). The mine operated until 1982. The time of change in the strategic orientation of the main investor must have influenced not only the residents of Butte but also the employees and managerial staff of companies located in that town. Decay, crisis, and loss of former prospects are clearly reflected in the photograph that may be seen as a picture of times of decline with previous rules of aesthetics and ethics being questioned and rejected.

The interior in the photograph is almost ruined. Electric wires and a bare bulb hang from the ceiling, and the room is untidy, even if documents on the desk are partly organized. The individual behind the desk seems to be embarrassed with his current environment. The portrait hung on the wall presumably depicts the firm's founder: smiling, looking confidently into the future, he echoes the remote glorious past of the business. That past stands in contrast to the present condition of the office.

In the discussed example, echoes of the past create an extremely meaningful and overwhelming atmosphere of nostalgia. The climate of the photograph provokes constructing possible hypothetical narratives, especially if the story

Table 4.9 Meaning of time as reflected in photographs and paintings

Time	Photographs	Paintings
Windows on the world	14.3%	50.0%
Passing time	0	25.0%
Longing for the next step	14.3%	25.0%
Memory of the past	71.4%	0

Source: Authors own elaboration

told is viewed from the perspective of frustration revealed by the face of the man portrayed and the local context in Butte, described above. It is a story of failure, bankruptcy of a place and idea, of the end of a project with its proud beginning recollected by memories of the figure depicted in the portrait on the wall.

Also in the case of time perspective, there are distinct differences between photographic material and painting and graphic material.

Photographs are characterized by a historical perspective, while projecting oneself into the future; opening up new horizons can be seen in paintings and graphics. In the former, the case is illustrated by accessories seen in portraits, such as photographs hung on office walls and presumably depicting the firm's founders. In the latter, a perspective going beyond 'here and now', seeking something more than current affairs, can be manifested both literally and metaphorically, through a 'window on the world', like in Hopper's *Office in a Small City* or Nevinson's *View from the Office Window*.

The differences between the nature of content communicated in paintings and that communicated in photographs are summarized in the code clouds shown in Figures 4.4 and 4.5. While the dominant semantic category in both sets is 'clothing convention', the paintings give importance to such categories as 'papers', 'standardization', 'contrasts and duplicity', 'indifference', and 'influential actors' (Figure 4.3).

On the other hand, the photographs show directed sight, calm, confidence of the figures portrayed as well as concentration and domination (Figure 4.4).

The code clouds allow to observe changing dynamics of artwork and photographic material. The condition of a minimum occurrence frequency of certain codes in material reveals that the photographs are paradoxically characterized by greater thematic intensity than paintings. For example, the set of photographs contains more than 20 codes with a minimum occurrence frequency of 5, while the set of paintings contain only 12 such codes; this may result from a greater number of elements in the former set. However, this relation is reversed, if also codes with a single occurrence are considered. Then, the code cloud of painting and graphic material is conceptually richer, although the set is smaller. The first observation results from the quantitative difference between photographic and painting material, the former being greater in number. A limit set on the code cloud, requiring a certain minimum occurrence frequency of specific concepts – that is, removing categories that are 'statistically' insignificant, characteristic, and typical of one or two artistic

Figure 4.3 Cloud of emergent codes, paintings and graphics (frequency 1, a limit of 25 codes)

Source: Authors own elaboration

Figure 4.4 Cloud of emergent codes, photographs (frequency 1, a limit of 25 codes)

Source: Authors own elaboration

representations – results in highlighting dominant discourse. On the other hand, inclusion of all codes is used to reveal rare narratives found in painting material that is open to multiple interpretations, rich in nuances and threads.

Dominant narratives give an incomplete picture due to the very fact of their prevalence. To achieve a more holistic view on representations of the world of organizations from an aesthetic perspective, rare narratives have to be included, and a synthesis of the prominent and the obvious must be complemented by considering the latent. An integrated code cloud, showing the nature of both paintings, graphics and photographs, indicates elements typical of dominant narratives.

A typology of figures – that is, domination, concentration, calm, elegance, confidence; stereotypes, disclosed by the clothing convention; community exemplified by a team; organizational phenomena illustrated by a systematic approach; and contrasts and duplicity – gives examples of dominant narratives. Their elements are shown as codes in Figure 4.5. Less common narratives (of endangered and looser communities, of travelling businessman) are not shown in the codecloud.

4.2.2 Player, official, homo liber

Who is the figure depicted in a work? It is both an individual, living in time and space, and an illustration of a social type. The figure portrayed happens to fit in both categories: the artist depicts an individual flesh and blood, but also a representative of a class, caste, group, or organization.

Figure 4.5 Integrated cloud of emergent codes. Dominant narratives

Source: Authors own elaboration

Businesspeople represented in artworks and photographs are classified as an official, a player, and a homo liber, with the type of player prevailing in representations (Chart 4.12).

Werner Sombart observed that the Western European entrepreneur combines two elements: an element of madness, risk (completely absent in the role of an official) and the element of calculation, reason (Merton, 1982). He writes:

> To my mind, the best picture of the modern capitalistic undertaker is that which paints him as the combination of two radically different natures in one person. Like Faust, he may say that two souls dwell within his breast; unlike Faust's, however, the two souls do not wish to be separated, but rather, on the contrary, desire to work harmoniously together. The one is the undertaker (not in the more limited sense of capitalistic undertaker, but quite generally), and the other is the trader.
>
> (idem, 2010, p. 32)

The contents of different functions combined in the activity of a capitalist entrepreneur include mission, a task performed in the external world and thus requiring the cooperation of others to be completed on the one hand, and appraising all activities and all conditions with a view to their money value, aiming at profitable business, on the other hand. The latter trait is characteristic of a merchant (trader) who differs from an entrepreneur by changing orientation, objectives and activities. An entrepreneur represents a constant factor,

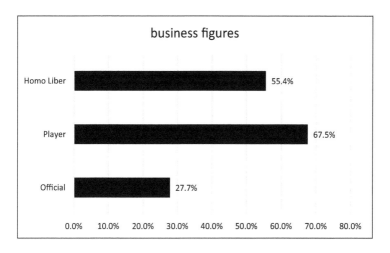

Chart 4.12 Key business figures

Source: Authors own elaboration

systematically endeavours to fulfil the mission accepted. Consequently, as Sombart puts it, 'the entrepreneur creates the rhythm while the trader – the melody in the capitalist musical work. The entrepreneur is the weft and the trader is the warp in the capitalist fabric' (Sombart, 2010, pp. 159–160).

This is illustrated by the type of business figure that we termed the 'player'. The player, participant in bids, coalitions, alliances, with his reflection that may be interpreted in terms of mindfulness, and his emotional reserve, co-creates the organization and saturates it with his personal traits. The player adapts to the circumstances, used to acting under conditions of diversity, characterized by eccentricity, astuteness, but emotionally calm, far from empathy, from understanding problems of others and considering another point of view. Examples of an insensitive, calculating, or even ruthless attitude towards others, driven by maximizing profits, are known in the visual arts and artistic literature (Reymont, 2020). The player is also aggressive, pushy, astute, duplicitous and confident, dogged, and haughty. These traits give the player a psychological advantage over potential opponents and make similarly behaving individuals form a social type known in numerous cultures. Social researchers, like Joseph Schumpeter, also observe that the entrepreneur is characterized by a certain narrowness of horizons. Schumpeter argues that economic success elevates entrepreneurs in social hierarchy. However, they lack cultural tradition and knowledge of forms, and frequently behave in society like social climbers (Schumpeter, 1960, p. 148). The entrepreneur is not a sophisticated intellectual or professed aesthete but someone who sees things invisible to others (Lavoi, 1994, pp. 48–49). Heilbroner commented on the figure of entrepreneur created by Schumpeter as a strange portrait, a mixture of someone driven by the instinct of workmanship on the one hand and by the predatory drive on the other hand (Heilbroner, 1993, pp. 263–264).

Paintings and photographs seem to confirm this picture of the player. Moreover, it happens that the unusual capability of spotting opportunities where others cannot see anything, or considering options that almost everyone else regards as impossible, lead not only to reflection, thought, weighing chances but also to thoughtlessness or simply fixation. The player may risk, bet heavily on business outcomes, and consequently may make wrong calculations and lose. The risk of failure is inherent in business; hence, we include in this category of figure such characteristics as frustration or depression that also appear in the analysed representations.

In a tiny, at first sight, office with intensely green walls, a figure wearing a blue suit is standing in an upright posture behind a simple wooden desk.[34] Shown in three-quarter, he seems to look attentively at the spectator. Large eyes with irises directed at an acute angle to the left carefully assess the situation. The sharp look is underlined by equally sharp facial features: a prominent straight nose whose line harmoniously combines with the eyebrow arch. The figure holds documents in hand, maybe just picked from the desk, on which a rather enormous telephone 'corresponds' to a calendar and a clock hung along the same vertical line on the opposite wall. Everything is very tidy there, also in terms of composition, with verticals marked by the figure and the calendar below a clock, and a horizontal marked by the line of the desktop. But it is the man's look that principally attracts attention. A look with a hint of craftiness, fox-like cunning, astuteness. According to our categories, *The Businessman Max Roesberg*, painted by Otto Dix (1891–1969) in 1922 is undoubtedly a player who will estimate risks and take purposeful steps to use the opportunities he identifies with his keen sight.

The work follows the rules of realism, specifically those proposed by the Neue Sachlichkeit (New Objectivity) movement. The figure is depicted in an office packed with a number of artefacts – attributes of his profession; he is standing stiffly, squeezed into clothes resembling a uniform rather than a suit, but undoubtedly confirming his identification and identity. The painting's colouring composed of cool shades of green and blue may allude to the colours of banknotes. The face of the figure seems to express a guaranteed win. Although his suit is an attribute of his profession, it gives his entire figure an aura of rigidity, emphasized by the clearly drawn lines and verticals, along the back of his head, and his vertically dropped arm. The figure makes the impression of being squeezed into his suit with its stiff collar, and those clothes do not seem comfortable. This is business wear that does not indicate an upper-class but a professional status. The businessman is set in a significant temporal perspective – 'here and now', at the current moment, which is symbolized by the clock reminding of the passage of time, although the calendar also introduces the perspective of planning and projecting oneself into the future (Kalinka, 1885). Is the player a timeless type of business figure? Are universal characteristics revealed in different representations of the player created over two centuries?

Here is a room with bronze walls free from any decoration, there is a man in sideview sitting on a plain wooden chair and wearing brown clothes with a tight, close-fitting, high, white collar around his neck. He attentively looks at the spectator. With his head eccentrically tilted to the right and irises directed at an acute angle to the left, he is carefully appraising the person in his view, as if estimating the significance of a potential business partner or contractor. His clothes seem comfortable, suitable for performing daily duties. Also this man holds some documents in hand. A minimalist colour palette and the absence of detail in the space where the figure is set enable the spectator to fully focus attention on the man, and attention is most attracted by his look – intriguing and mysterious. Behind it, there is a special kind of cunning, astuteness of someone who knows more than he is willing to tell, who has his secrets, and plays his strategic matches with confidence, complete self-control and calm. This player is Thomas Staniforth depicted in a 18th-century portrait by Joseph Wright of Derby (1734–1797).[35]

The man portrayed seems to get in contact with the spectator; his face emanates not only calm confidence and eccentricity but also a kind of energy and the intention to communicate. The businessman in the portrait who was famous in his times, and engaged in what was euphemistically termed 'overseas trade',[36] makes an impression of someone who asks questions knowing in advance the answers. The figure emerges from the background in clothes forming a rather uniform colour area that seems to be closely related to the background. There is no contrast or clear, strong separation from the background. The colour of the environment amalgamates with the colour of clothes, and the face is the only lit element. This close connection of the figure with his surroundings provokes a thought about a situation where someone is an integral part of their environment that may even absorb them. The bronze and brown colouring may be associated, for example, with dirtying one's hands in business, and the figure's clothes, although conventional, is surely business wear – certainly not formal dress. The position of his crossed, resting hands suggests relaxation after a closed deal. The figure definitely is 'on home turf', may indulge in a little nonchalance – his posture speaks for his domination and being the master of a situation. He is undoubtedly the 'owner of the stage' in his own 'theatre', and his facial expression can be verbalized as 'didn't I tell you'. Cunning and astuteness are the characteristics that may be identified in his look that simultaneously seems to assess whether the 'other party' – interlocutor, business partner or contractor – is a worthy opponent and what are his thoughts and advantages.

The nature of business that the portrayed man works in is not illustrated in the painting in any way. However, the clothes seem to indicate rather regular daily work than ostentatious affluence or a high social status. The portrait that represents facial features without flattering may suggest that the artist depicted with full awareness the characteristics of the middle class built on trade and not the elegance of aristocracy (www.tate.org.uk/art/artworks/wright-thomas-staniforth-of-darnall-co-york-t00794, accessed: 3.08.23)

A player can also be recognized in the subject of a portrait depicting figures on a trading day at the Paris Stock Exchange: financier and art collector Ernest May, with an associate leaning over his shoulder (*Portraits at the Stock Exchange*, Edgar Degas, ca. 1878–1879).[37]

This study for an oil painting held at Musée d'Orsay is described as observation of the subject with a distinct distance, maybe due to a certain aversion to the world of finance, attributed to Degas. The group portrayed seems to be typical, considering representations of the social class and style characteristic of that period. The artist's negative attitude towards the world of finance can be seen in the way he depicted the characters – the main subject looking much older that he actually was, the absence of certain traits in the figures shown in the background, as if deprived of importance and individual meaning and being used only to illustrate activity and busyness typical of a security trading place (www.musee-orsay.fr/en/artworks/portraits-la-bourse-1145, accessed: 3.08.23, www.metmuseum.org/art/collection/search/436154, accessed: 3.08.23).

The clothes of the men portrayed indicate that they belong to a certain social class. The figure providing information is depicted using another colour scheme compared to the other figures and the background. That colour scheme is rather contrasting, which may be interpreted in terms of a kind of opposition. Is it an opponent or an informant who delivers a confidential message?

A typical young businessman at the London Stock Exchange portrayed by Emil Otto Hoppe in 1937 displays a considerable visual similarity to the Parisian players. We see an extremely elegant young man who is fully aware of his growing or maybe already attained position and importance. There is also another figure in the frame, in the middle ground; a man with an attentive but tired look; wearing less elegant clothes. He seems to belong to another social stratum. The difference between the two figures can be described as that between the elite and middle class. Despite elegance or even refinement of his clothes, the young businessman illustrates certain standardization typical of the business elite community, people of success.

His posture suggests considering an option, decision to be made, or consequences of a decision that was already made, but surely must have been right. His hand on hip, elbow directed outward, and upright posture predict resolute and even aggressive action.

The official is completely another type of person. He is characterized by meticulousness and standardization of action. The official has to behave in a predictable way, follow procedures. The official may be indifferent – he has no emotional ties with the funds he manages on someone else's behalf. His involvement in his office mission may also be limited – this is not his own business. The official adapts to his precisely defined role, although as a figure model offers a limited number of interpretations. His role and position seem to be fixed, dictated by rules, predictable. He is a living emanation of the Weber's ideal type of bureaucracy; such officials can be seen in accounting firms or revenue offices.

Officials or clerks are portrayed by Pieter de Josselin de Jong (1861–1906) in his work *In the office*.[38] The two foreground figures are fully concentrated on their task that is absolutely central to the depicted situation, as indicated by the use of chiaroscuro. Light draws full attention to the task, leaving in shadow everything else, including a figure barely emerging from the background who seems to inspect or formally supervise work done by others but still remains in the background of the main scene. The main character in the picture is keeping his left hand on an inspected document entry and diligently copying and recording that entry with his right hand. The position of his taut fingers indicates his concentration, and although the situation characterized by a strong hierarchy, it is a form of teamwork in which an assistant works together with his colleague. The painting illustrates the relation of ownership indicated by the mysterious figure of supervisor depicted on the right of the composition in the middle ground, in opposition to the employees who diligently perform their duties. Paradoxically, the hierarchical aspect of the entire scene is underlined by a bored and unoccupied figure situated in a distant recession plane, being perhaps an applicant or trainee, not permitted to actually work, required to observe and learn. Boredom and indifference betrayed by his face may be considered emblematic of bureaucratic, petrified official structures where activity consists in imitating rather than in creating. The imitative nature of work is also epitomized by the depicted task performed by the main character who mechanically is copying data from one record to another.

Figures who represent the type of official evoke associations with bureaucracy which is illustrated in *Untitled (Office Workers)* from 1950, by Carl M. Schultheiss (1885–1961), an immigrant to America, born in Nuremberg. The etching can be described as an emblematic illustration of a system known in management theory as Taylorism. It represents strict division of work, allocation of people to workstations, a sequence of individual tasks and their synthesis, with simultaneous absent or minimal interaction and cooperation.

The ladies who work in a schematically, geometrically organized office space, represented, in aesthetic terms, in a planar composition, are turned away from each other, and focused on their own tasks. The artwork emphasizes a rigid internal framework of the work environment, and consequently a similar organizational framework. The space is closed, creating cramped conditions. The figures are packed together. They are also characterized by a physical similarity and an imposed format revealed by their clothes and standardization of the interior. This provokes a thought about Merton's discussion of the influence of bureaucracy on personality of people involved (1982). He writes:

> A formal, rationally organized social structure involves clearly defined patterns of activity. . . , every series of actions is functionally related to the purposes of the organization. . . . man is to a very important degree controlled by his social relations to the instruments of production. . . . the bureaucratic structure exerts a constant pressure upon the official to be 'methodical, prudent, disciplined.' The efficacy . . . depends ultimately upon infusing . . . participants with appropriate attitudes and sentiments.
>
> (Merton, 1982, pp. 255–259)

The figures depicted in the artworks also appear as *homines liberi*. The Latin word *liber* means someone who is unconstrained, unrestrained, unworried, outspoken, free, open, politically autonomous – in a word, an antonym of 'slave' (Kumaniecki, 1976). It is someone who is independent and sovereign, which seems to be reflected in the status of middle-class representatives who perform the role of employers, and possess resources giving them existential and thus intellectual independence of the state's structures and public authorities. In our paintings and photographs, these people are well-off, cheerful, cordial and plump, physically attractive, calm, elegant, sometimes adhering to the hedonistic concept of happiness. Some works may be indicative of lustfulness of the people portrayed, and surely of their satisfaction and pride in their achieved status of wealthy individuals. The portrait of Henry Crispe, discussed above, shows a man whose appearance indicative of hedonistic habits seems to embody those traits.

The homo liber is someone who enjoys freedom resulting from their agency – from being 'on home turf'. This is indicated, for example, by a sitting position with a hand freely lowered or a cheerful disposition seen in the smile. However, the portrait of bankers by Walker Evans show something more than freedom, namely nonchalance, confidence that an attitude can be shown to others, without regard to strict rules of etiquette, saying, 'I am what I am and no convention is binding on me'.

This type of attitude can also be displayed in offices where businessmen receive their guests while sitting on their desks, or in public space where a moment of conversation in front of a building during a lunch break, or a casual meeting on the way to negotiations provide an opportunity form manifesting the same kind of freedom, satisfaction in life, cheerfulness, smile and confidence given by the professional and presumably social status achieved.

There are two gentlemen standing and leaning against a wall, perhaps of a bank or tall office building. Partly turned towards each other, with one elbow resting on the building's sill, and the other hand in pocket or joyfully put on hip. One of them put his left foot slightly forward, as if in the at-ease position, the other has his legs crossed, right foot put on left ankle – this is a more comfortable stance. Loose suites, relaxed hands, hats on heads and a broad smile on the face of one of them. These are *Two Businessmen in Hats Talking on Street, Florida* by Walker Evans.[39]

Representing the type of *homines liberi*, they emanate calm and satisfaction, and the spectator, involved in the situation depicted, shares freedom from worry and joy of life, which seems not only to fill that short moment captured in the photograph but also to be a trait of deep identities of the men portrayed.

Thus, people of the organization appear as individuals with a variety of personality traits, multi-dimensional, experiencing emotions, but also remarkably persistent and calm. These multi-dimensional characteristics are a warning against the lure of far-reaching generalizations, against generalizing surveys that comprise representative samples and that surely are not capable of capturing those qualities that are revealed when analysing pictures rather than questionnaire choices or market trends.

4.2.3   *Picture of the organization trapped in stereotypes*

A stereotype is a model of reality, an ungrounded generalization emphasizing a single characteristic or trait, but also a cognitive construct that is used to comprehend the complex structure of social, economic, or organizational life. Stereotypes, such as depicting organizational life from the perspective of roles performed by a boss and a receptionist or assistant, the roles once assigned[40] to gender, certainly lead to a simplified picture of the social world of organizations; still, this type of perception is found in the artworks described.

It is night, obviously a late hour. There are only two people in the office – a man sitting behind a desk and a woman standing farther and slightly on the side, with her face turned towards him, and reaching for some documents or files in a drawer. The man, her boss, without a shadow of doubt, is not looking in her direction and seems to be fully absorbed in reading a letter. The woman here is evidently his subordinate, although we cannot tell anything more about their relationship. The man wears a suit typical of supervisors at office work, the woman – fairly elegant, conventional clothes which nevertheless clearly disclose her figure and underline her charm. This is the depiction of clothes or dress that provokes a thought about a stereotypical image of office or organizational conventions. Hopper's *Office at Night* proposes principally a narrative of stereotypical organizational roles where a man is the boss and a woman performs ancillary tasks. We also see women in an office depicted by Carl M. Schultheiss who represent in his *Untitled (Office Workers)* a fragment of office space divided into smaller areas formed in an almost geometric way by workstations arranged for individual employees who are busy with typing, calculating something, searching in documents, or recording a telephone conversation. In a word, these employees perform simple administrative tasks. The figures look similar, are simply standardized, especially regarding their clothes. The point is that all of them are women, and also this picture echoes the stereotype of organizational roles with ladies assigned to do administrative jobs, and not to managing. A woman, if finally portrayed in the role of *businesswoman*, is caricatured and lampooned as a personification of chaos, lack of self-control and incapability of managing situation, exaggeration, and eccentricity, as in the painting by Peter Saul.[41]

The portraying of almost all characters in the same way, wearing similar clothes, provokes an irresistible thought about a perpetuated stereotype of 'man of the organization' or 'people of the organization'. Undoubtedly, the standardization of clothing and the convention of 'bearing' is a dominant narrative in representations of business figures who are perceived as aesthetically and visually formatted, but a stereotyped perception of business also echoes in rare narratives that perpetuate a definite and polarized view on male and female roles in business, even making the latter a target for satire.

Today, stereotypes concerning the world of organized economic activity[42] are revealed in the perception of entrepreneur and business figures in negative categories: as dishonest, cunning, and sly, which may be associated with viewing the origins of big fortunes in terms of political involvement and taking advantage of connections and privileged relationships. Tensions between top-level managers and ordinary employees result in creating a picture of the businessperson as an exploiter or simply a Dickensian capitalist for whom people work while he or she enjoys the pleasures of an affluent lifestyle, demonstrating superiority of his or her financial status. However, the visual stereotype of a businessman wearing a conventional suit has gradually changed. That business wear evokes increasingly frequent associations not with business but rather with customer service as an attribute of officials and salesmen, not of managers or entrepreneurs. Interestingly, certain stereotypes of self-perception are created in the community of companies and corporations. Those stereotypes include believing in the existence of a firm visual stratification that reflects the formal organizational hierarchy – a deep belief that it is appropriate at a certain level of positions occupied to be a consumer of specific brands, for example of cars, which turns into a kind of perceptual aid used to help others correctly evaluate someone's achievements. Such intra-community stereotypes also include the belief in insincerity of businesspeople who allegedly create for themselves an image that is expected by others, and not necessarily real; consequently, they must be posing and pretending – hiding their true faces. The last question is clearly recognizable in motifs referring to a face of Janus.

4.2.4 Knights in a circle

The represented world of organizations is usually, except few abstractionist works concerning this topic, filled with figures. In most cases, these human figures are represented in a naturalistic manner either in figurative painting or in photographs, although there are also symbolic or caricatured figures. However, regardless of the way of representation, attention is attracted by the varying nature of their co-appearance with others. The community of peoples represented may take various forms depending on the element by which it is united. A classical form of community is undoubtedly a team – that is, a group of people who are united by a goal that they jointly wish to achieve.

The clerks in the work by de Jong, like the ladies in an office, typists in *Untitled (Office workers)*, are focused on tasks that finally are to be combined to achieve a common goal, which is stronger indicated in the composition by de Jong, where the figures are slightly turned towards each other – their heads are leaned over common documentation. We see a room resembling rather a chancery or counting room than an office in a modern understanding of that word. Parallel to the painting frame, there is the side of a very long desktop, with its perspective representation defining the room's depth. The clerks sitting along the desktop are focused on their tasks. A grey-haired gentleman in a neat frock coat is diligently copying some data from a sheet of paper to a large record. The extremely taut fingers of his left hand are resting on a document, indicating a line of data to avoid mistakes. His glasses, lowered half through his nose, are carefully following the movement of a quill. The figure is shown in profile, with another employee close behind him, sitting slightly sideways to the line of the desktop, writing something with equal concentration in another record, leaning his right elbow firmly on the counter.

The last in a row, a young boy, is sitting unoccupied, leaning his chin on hand but looking at his older colleagues – learning by observation – there is place also for him, a trainee or assistant, in this bureaucratic world, supervised, we guess, by a mysterious figure who walks in shadow behind the clerks with his hand behind the back. Evenly distributed light clearly divides the room's space into a bright area with the desktop, documents, and clerks' faces, and a shadowed area with a figure turned back to us, a supervisor or perhaps the owner of the counting office. The configuration of characters in a row, beginning with the one who presumably performs the most important tasks, then his colleague, ending with a man who has no important task and is learning from watching others, can be associated with a line organizational structure and process-oriented work design where one person's performance affects others. Undoubtedly, the clerks depicted work for someone and on something, and thus achieving a common goal and forming a team, and their work shows no sign of alienation.

In the case of *Office Workers*, this is less evident, because there is no interaction between the figures. Certainly, they jointly occupy an office and implicitly work on a common outcome, but almost all of them are turned back or side to each other and have clearly separated workstations, unlike the clerks who are sitting at one desk resembling a production line. Presumably, the typists also work for someone and on something, but the nature of their jobs is different. They are performing their tasks in an alienated way, as if each of them created something for a different supervisor or client. There is no character with a clear executive or managing role; thus, this form of loose community may be seen as a counterbalance to a coherent team with evident signs of cooperation.

The 1947 painting by Jacob Lawrence, *The Businessmen*, represents yet another situation. Against an orange and amaranth background of a wall with no detail. we see a group of five figures sitting in a circle. They are sitting on plain chairs – dark-skinned characters in dark, loose suits – downward shoulder lines, bald heads leaning forward indicate concentration shared by the entire group in a rather depressing atmosphere. Obviously, they have got a problem. They are holding papers, partly dropped on the floor, in between them, next to their feet. The documents are distinguished by their yellow and beige colours, shining bright between dark areas that form the figures who seem to be gathered around a bonfire, if seeking farther associations with the general layout of the entire composition. Under the arm of one figure, in the hand of another and on the floor, there is an additional lively coloured and most expressive element – red document folders. The figure on the left dropped his hat under his char and is browsing documents – seems to be thinking constructively. The figure on the right is making a palmface gesture – apparently submitting to frustration. Both figures – the constructive and the worried – are sitting opposite one another, showing a contradictory nature of their approaches to the problem.

There is an evident context of a threat that has made them unite. That union is depicted by arranging the figures in a circle. Sitting, they lean over a common set of documents. People may sit around a bonfire or a table, but the focal point for the meeting in this case is formed by papers as a symbol of knowledge or information. The configuration of characters in a circle also suggests their equal status, and this impression is reinforced by their standardized look or even an imposed format, both in terms of their shape – they are represented rather schematically in a simplified way – and in terms of their clothes and identical colour accents. They are modern knights completely devoted to solving a problem and a common cause. The main colour accents in the painting are laid on documents and folders. The reaction of the figures to the problem is the sole element that differentiates them. One is making the palmface gesture, displaying frustrating reflection; another has given up; yet another is still fighting – reading documents, taking a rational attitude. They may be entrepreneurs who are trying to save a project that is falling apart, seeking a solution or valuable information in falling-apart documents, or perhaps slaves to a procedure, subject to written instructions. Let us allow another tempting interpretation. The absence of a table and the documents spread on the floor, people leaning forward on their chairs – all this makes an impression of a certain disorder, and thus an informal nature of the meeting, perhaps accompanied by hurry. This can be the matter of lawful access to information sought by the characters or maybe the momentary and temporary nature of the situation they are facing.

Whatever details are added to this tale, we can obviously see a closely integrated team – modern knights in a concentric circle that defines the field of their cooperation and responsibility.

This modernist painting is part of the series *In the Heart of the Black Belt* commissioned by Walker Evans for *Fortune* magazine and based on sketches drawn by the author during a journey across the Southern United States. The picture of dark-skinned characters reveals a cubist manner, a simplified, even tending towards abstractionism, form of human figures set in a reduced colour scheme. The colouring dynamics nicely contrast with the characters' seriousness and calm. Although the works of Lawrence are commonly considered to be set in a socio-political context of racial questions, they should be viewed as interdisciplinary and transcendent. This may be confirmed by the fact that in our analysis of *The Businessmen*, we observed no racial connotation, and this reveals a humanist potential of the work for crossing the boundaries of standard expression (www.sothebys.com/en/auctions/ecatalogue/2018/contemporary-art-evening-sale-n09932/lot.18.html, accessed: 3.08.23).

4.2.5   *The communities of the wealthy, endangered, and losers*

Depictions and illustrations of the world of organizations naturally represent characters in the context of teams, and this is actually confirmed by the frequency of that code (41.7%) in the category of 'community'. However, looking at paintings and drawings that disclose the perception of business and the organization, we can clearly see that groups aggregating people in the pictures are not homogeneous and differ. Considering rare narratives in coded visual material, we recognize the importance of marginal communities shown in artworks. These are the communities of the endangered and losers, as contrasted with the communities of the wealthy. The most obvious illustration of this phenomenon is given in *Charity Organization Society* by Tonks.[43]

We see a sad figure, depressed by the filling of guilt, standing on an object resembling a goods-weighing scale. In the background, on the wall, a table of nutrients is displayed. It seems that the 'defendant' is being assessed and charged with a kind of negligence and carelessness, either of himself or others. He is guilty of something, most probably of his poverty and low social status. The work undoubtedly shows a fairly distinct confrontation. The poor man is faced with opposition based on the absence of sympathy for helplessness. This is illustrated by the group of adversaries situated on the right of the composition behind the principal judge. Attention is also drawn to the figure of a slightly smiling woman at the right top of the composition who signals with her posture distance from the entire situation. This is distance from the other members of the society – the woman slightly turns away from the group, and her posture directed sideways indicates a lack of engagement. She is the only one to have a kind smile, but this cannot change the fact that she also distances herself from the man being assessed, which is recognizable in the delicately nonchalant gesture of her dropped hand, whose movement may be perceived as slightly disrespectful.

However, it seems that she distances herself not from the 'group of adversaries' but rather from the situation as a whole. A conclusion may be drawn that a direct confrontation with poverty and failure causes aggression or indifference. The community of the wealthy donors is clearly confronted here with those who stand 'on the other side'.

For a full understanding of *Charity Organization Society*, knowledge of the historical context is essential. Charitable societies were treated as a means to provide those who deserved it with the skills and opportunities necessary to personally overcome a problematic situation. It was believed that donations that did not contribute to making the recipient more self-reliant and competent were a waste of donors' funds and harmed the recipient. The key factor in the operation of charitable societies was to professionally and institutionally distinguish those who deserved assistance from those who did not deserve help, and this was achieved by way of diligent judgement and assessment of each case. This process is shown in the described work that even by its composition may evoke associations with a court room with a judge in its centre, turning with his menacing hand gesture to the assessed, who, importantly, is standing on a weighing scale, and behind the judge, on the right of the composition, indignation or perhaps disapproval is expressed by the jury – representatives of high society and benefactors of charitable societies.

The expression of guilt on the face of the 'defendant' may reflect the essential philosophical trait of chartable societies, which presents poverty as a consequence of the moral imperfection of an individual.

In the 19th century, institutions designed to provide aid were based on voluntary and private rather than government or ecclesiastic charity. Promoting such an approach is characteristic of Victorian England, and the *London Society for Organising Charitable Relief and Repressing Mendicity* (*Charity Organisation Society*) was established in 1869 in response to the criticism of providing assistance without properly estimating who deserved it and who did not (Cold as Charity: philanthropy and the notion of the 'undeserving poor', https://whyphilanthropymatters.com/article/cold-as-charity/, accessed: 3.08.23).

The community of losers, indicated in the depiction of a charitable society where a representative of that community is confronted with the community of the wealthy, is clearly shown in the lithograph *Employment Office* by Jolan Gross-Bettelheim (1900–1972), a modernist work from 1936. This expressive work evokes associations with an interrogation room. This effect is reinforced by combining sharp contrasts in chiaroscuro with a striped, black-and-white suit of one of the characters, resembling a prison uniform. The graphic in the black and white colour scheme is relatively linear, making an impression of ranking. Ranking is done by the vertical stripes on the clothes of people lined up in a row. This impression is reinforced by the slant line defined by a counter behind which are standing and on which are leaning the figures of the unemployed, a line additionally emphasized by the lines of forearms resting on the counter. The slant of the counter marks a hierarchy – it is a queue where someone stands before someone else. This impression would not be made if the counter line was a simple horizontal. The graphic also lacks any movement. There reigns stillness, stagnation, which augment the impression of despair felt by the figures packed together in the work's centre. Here, packing together is a symbol of the absence of opportunities and chances in life, and the standard way of creating figure forms – they are separated from their environment using similar distinct lines – makes them being perceived as objects. They are petitioners brought to the employment office by their needs and difficult living conditions. These characters are anonymous and simply formatted by their bad luck. Their faces are expressing frustration. Perhaps they have visited this place before, and this makes them ashamed of their fruitless efforts of their misfortune. Perhaps, they are there for the first time, which is also connected with the feeling of shame, admitting that they have come to seek a kind of aid.

This type of community sense differs from that characteristic of the community of the wealthy. Namely, the similarity of situation forms a stratum of people who experience the same circumstances or position, but they remain anonymous to each other and have no feeling of common interest. They are standing next to each other but not together, which is clearly seen in the work's composition.

The absence of common interest that could unite people in their activity while also building a community around situational conditions is also visible in the 1935 work with a quite provocative title *Organizational Advances* by Albert Potter (1903–1937), a Russian-born immigrant to America. We see an aesthetically degraded neighbourhood, a space limited in the foreground by a fence with a garbage can in front of it, and on the other side, a far perspective of a rich city with a horizon line marked by skyscrapers, probably office buildings. That far perspective defines a horizon of future events – perhaps dreams or ambitions or past events – perhaps former places of making deals and doing business, now lost, and brings the figures depicted to their current place, somewhere on the periphery away from the rich business district but close to a rubbish tip. The distinct line of perspective that organizes the work's space sets its frame, which may be metaphorically treated as a life framework in which the group of characters is packed together. We see depressed faces, dropped mouth corners, avoiding meeting someone else's eyes, lowered eyes – those people are brought there by their needs, poverty, and necessity to work, like in *Employment Office*. This is a group of alienated people moving chaotically. It can be concluded from the composition that the movements of the figures carrying advertisements for various firms and products are not correlated. Their paths are chaotic; they are jostling, perhaps shoving, among others, self-centred, with no interaction. No common direction is set.

The work can be understood as a metaphor for the market as a battlefield, both for companies and for people, although the message is fairly complex and offers multiple levels of interpretation.

Attention is caught by the figure in the centre of the composition, who may still be living or not, evoking associations with death and at the same time carrying a slogan advertising foodstuffs. Interpreted from the perspective of a social message, the artwork can be understood as a manifestation of a dysfunctional nature of the market that forces the poor and less resourceful to work for the wealthy who have achieved success. This is a tale of unequal socio-economic statuses. But also, another narrative can be constructed, considering that the subject of the work is organizations, as suggested by its title. Then, the work becomes an illustration of greed in business, flattering customers with its advertising slogans and using the circumstances – for example, unscrupulously exploiting people forced to do badly paid work.

A compositional similarity can be perceived in the two artworks showing communities of the endangered and losers, in the form of frames that close the compositions in both cases. In *Organizational Advances*, this is a fence being a thin line separating the characters from a worse line, from falling into complete degradation, and ending at the metaphorical 'rubbish tip'. In the case of *Employment Office*, the counter at which the applicants are standing separates them from a better life – we certainly can guess that there is someone behind the counter who can open their way to solving life problems.

4.2.6 Travelling entrepreneur

The frequently used metaphors of 'road' or 'journey' with reference to life are so meaningful that they also appear in representations of the world of organizations and its people, even if this is not a dominant picture but rather a rare narrative. However, the picture of a businessperson, an entrepreneur, as a traveller who needs navigation tools in a turbulent environment – tools that are useful in defending oneself against threats but also provide support and assistance in decision-making and managing business development – is a promising picture and allows to observe that the identity of business figures is, or at least was in the past, more complex and complicated than it might seem.

The symbol leading to this reflection is a walking staff or stick appearing as attributes of business figures, artefacts with which those people are portrayed, in addition to more obvious accessories typical of office work, such as a fountain pen, telephone, or ubiquitous documents.

The impressive figure of Sir Benjamin Truman,[44] depicted during a walk, perhaps across his estate, shows him as a traveller holding in hand a staff that might serve as a convenient walking aid but also as a tool used to remove stones in front of feet or explore bushes if the traveller wishes to depart from a well-trodden path.[45]

The portrait by Gainsborough commissioned by Truman was to decorate one of his houses,[46] which seems to correspond to the character of that figure, who displays in the described picture a thinly disguised contempt and a distinct feeling of superiority over the world around (www.tate.org.uk/art/artworks/gainsborough-sir-benjamin-truman-t02261, accessed: 3.08.23); after all, he is the owner of a brewing empire. As regards the colour scheme, the figure corresponds to his environment, constitutes its integral part, which makes the impression of harmony and may symbolize a firm position in the local community. The staff that he is holding is a tool for exercising power, as suits a man of action and decision, and is an extension of his hand. Simultaneously, the dominant and commanding character of the figure is mitigated by an elegant top hat he is holding in hand, perhaps in a gesture prepared for politely greeting someone who may casually be met on the way.

In more recent times, journeys made by businesspeople may have a varying nature. Sir Benjamin was perhaps depicted during an inspection of his estate. For today's businesspeople, most part of their organizational journey, understood literally rather than metaphorically (as, e.g., a journey upward in the organizational hierarchy of power), consists of more common commuting or business trips. It seems that this element of life is not worth special depiction, except for the purposes of documenting some emblematic or typical fragment of a broader social reality. However, photographs taken by Walker

Evans capture business figures also as ordinary pedestrians on their way to work. We see them in a casual conversation on the street (*Two Businessmen in Hats Talking on Street, Walker Evans, 1941, Two Businessmen: for the Series 'Dress'*), or heading alone for their offices with quick, steady steps after a lunch break, or carrying their lunch to be consumed in the office (*Business Man, Bridgeport, Connecticut*).[47]

The dominant aspect in all those photographs is the fleeting and everyday nature of the moment, without any element of celebrating the context or the character as such, as is the case in the portrait of Sir Benjamin.

While the photographs by Evans are inspired by the meaning of ordinary moments in everyday life and depict their reality, the 1948 drawing *A Walk to the Office* by Lucian Freud[48] (1922–2011), a representative of British figure painting, is an unreal projection – illustration of a fantasy story told by William Sansom in his novella *The Equilibriad*. The drawing depicts a man holding a handrail who is suddenly stopped by something invisible. The protagonist of the novella discovers one day that he is able to walk only at a 45-degree angle, and at the fleeting moment depicted in the drawing, he manages, despite his physical imperfection, to grasp a ball dropped by a little boy. However, the moment of joy quickly turns into consternation as the boy responds with a cry to the man's strange way of movement. The drawing is characterized by clarity, precision, unique contrastive use of dark and light tones (www.christies. com/lot/lot-lucian-freud-a-walk-to-the-office-5698846/?from=salesummery& intobjectid=5698846&lid=1&sc_lang=en&sid=9b6bf927-8bbd-49f8-a54b-6da744817962, accessed: 3.08.23).

The figure involuntarily shields himself with his hand, turning to the handrail that provides support in his unsteady walk. He cautiously takes a step forward, as if hesitating, feeling the ground. The man seems to be lost in his oversized suit, as if overwhelmed by his role, function, or situation;[49] his appearance might make the impression of nonchalance, but the clothes are simple and cheap, evoking associations with his background or social status. He is perhaps a promoted shop-floor worker or someone who recently attained a higher social status. Holding the handrail as a symbol of support needed, along with the worried facial expression and unsteady step, creates a clear message – a tale of someone who lacks confidence in their own qualities or capabilities and who tries to proceed, seeking every assistance available.

Although it is an illustration of a particular story, the sketch is open to multiple interpretations. We can consider how to interpret, in the context of today's reflection on interpersonal relationships, the framework story presented in the described drawing, telling about reactions to our limitations (*strange steps, a strange body*), regardless of the result of the efforts that we make and the success that we can achieve (*catching the ball*). It seems that the psychological context of this composition is created by reflection on the meaning of our limitations to the way we are perceived by others, despite our success and achievements.

4.2.7 Phenomena: the organization as a space of secrecy and contrasts

Let us note that 'phenomenon' means something that is observed to exist or happen, a fact or event. A phenomenon means also 'something unusual, extraordinary, something remarkable, unusual, unique' (Doroszewski, 1996–1997), finally, an 'apparition, dream vision, mare, illusion, spectre'[50] (Doroszewski, 1996, https://doroszewski.pwn.pl/haslo/zjawisko/ , accessed: 28.08.2023). 'Phenomenon' thus belongs to a fairly broad range of 'beings' between reality and illusion, fact and fiction, account and creation, and may include parts of all those shades. Phenomenon, being in our study the illustrated fact, event, situation from the life of organizations or people of organizations – is a category quite rich in meanings.

A phenomenon may mean secrecy. Wherever darkness appears – be it in a photograph or in a painting – there is a suggestion that something mysterious is happening, the picture hides a secret. The artist considers secrecy to be an aspect of the world of business, success, fortune. Chiaroscuro has a key role in depicting secrecy – the play between the brightly lit and evident and the hidden, dark, and implicit. Here we see a lit figure in the foreground, but the background is dark, perhaps even ominous. The figure emerges from that background; we can see some furniture, chair, or armchair, but not much more (see Thomas Staniforth of Darnall, Co. York, by Wright J., of Derby, in: www. tate.org.uk/art/artworks/wright-thomas-staniforth-of-darnall-co-york-t00794, 28.082023).

Photographs of people from General Electric and Lorillard Co., taken by Evans for *Fortune* magazine, show chief executives of big corporations emerging from shade, for example, with one half of their faces lit and the other secretly hidden from sight of the spectator.

Staying in a shadow, in addition to a purely artistic effect, may carry the symbolism of business secrets, not disclosing strategic plans, or illustrate the effect of surprise, frequently desirable for organizations.

Secrecy in the organizational context always takes some form of the unspoken. The effect may be achieved by the refined use of chiaroscuro, a classical means of artistic expression, and by creating an atmosphere, but secrecy may also be conveyed by introducing subtle hints of double meaning or creating situational areas of ambiguity.

For example, the painting by Edward Hopper *Office at Night* shows a modest office, as if arranged in an entrance area of a larger space, which may be indicated by the door, perhaps opening to a waiting room. There are two desks arranged opposite each other. It seems that the woman, who occupies the place across from her male boss, has just left her seat at the typewriter and is searching for documents in drawers with folders, standing in a position that indicates expecting an instruction or decision, with her look focused on her boss. The roles are very clearly defined here. The woman is a receptionist or assistant – she is standing, and the man is her boss – owner or the office – sitting behind a desk. The woman is attractive, wearing a close-fitting dress that underlines her figure. The boss is sitting, focused on documents, indifferent at the moment to his environment, but he is to decide when to break the silence and look at her. Eye contact is unilateral here, and the atmosphere is filled with expectation. It is a late-night hour.

It can easily be concluded from the intimate atmosphere of the painting that sets the scene showing joint work by a small team of two people in a tiny office occupied by a lawyer or private investigator – a scene bathed in light with warm colour shades and softness – that this is a story of certain secrecy. The unspoken, evidently existing in this picture, conceals the nature of the relationship between two people – which may be a purely professional relationship between two people who are forced to work late at night by a huge workload and tight deadlines. However, the space of the unspoken created by aesthetic, painter's means of expression introduces in the situation the context of secrecy and suggestion of possible multifaceted and complex relationships between the man and the woman in the painting.[51]

Another painting by Hopper, *New York Office*, from 1962 depicts an office at a street corner, with a woman in the foreground who is reading with deep concentration a letter or document. The woman's figure is lit, while the room behind her lies in darkness and shadow. Also this time, the artist portrayed a charming woman in an off-the-shoulder dress. It is not known what kind of letter she is reading. We guess that it is related to her job because the scene is set in an office and she is standing next to a desk, but maybe it is a private letter that she wanted to open away from their colleagues – a mysterious document and emptiness reinforcing an aura of secrecy and reflection. Recession of an office interior immersed in darkness, where in a far plane another person is seated, is marked only by a dark colour area but not defined by precise contour. It seems that the woman with a letter is standing in solitude in her environment where nothing is happening or moving. This impression is reinforced by an empty side road set in linear correlation with her. Chiaroscuro in the form of a very bright street lit by natural light contrasting with the dark office interior creates the impression of depth emphasized by one-point perspective strongly accentuated by the line of lamps. In an interpretation, this is an antithesis of viewing the organization as a flat structure and shows its spatial dimension. Distance is a dominant element of the picture. The office interior lost in darkness seems to be distant from the huge, bright window, which is emphasized by the difference in figure proportions. The woman with a letter distances herself from others, turning back to them and to her routines, presumably taking a break from work at her desk to focus on the message received.

A phenomenon that has an equally strong presence in paintings is contrast, duplicity, the boundary between the world of business and the environment, between social strata, poverty, and wealth. A contrast as a boundary between different worlds can be seen in the office of a charitable organization (*Charity Organization Society*), where the wealthy and the needy are standing opposite. The artwork by Tonks *Charity Organization Society* illustrates social contrasts that meet in an institutional approach to charity whereby funds donated by wealthy people of success, portrayed as a tight group on the right of the composition, are to be used to provide aid to the needy and poor, depicted on the left of the composition. This will happen according to a decision made by the judge, the central figure in the picture, whose task is to resolve who deserves and who does not deserve assistance.

The boundary between two worlds also appears in the form of limited space in which men carrying advertising boards are packed (*Organizational Advances*), pressed in between the horizon with the office district of a rich city and a fence with a garbage can behind it, and between the world of advertisements for attractive, young, healthy lifestyle and their economic misery.

A contrast or duplicity is an identity trait of a businessman as perceived by George Condo, giving his character a halved face, as if constructed from two halves that experience separate emotions. In *Businessmen* by George Condo, contrast is marked by the facial axis of symmetry. Either half seems to express its own feelings. One is calm – with the eye slightly narrowed, even cunning. The other half expresses horror and scream – with the eye wide open, staring in a sudden attack of fear or anger, and the mouth exposing teeth in an aggressive grimace. It seems that we see two personalities of a single character. It is a face of Janus that may explicitly illustrate duplicity or the face of a schizoid man indicating internal contradictions, embodying personality contrasts.[52]

Looking at the dual businessman, depicted by Condo in such a dreamlike way, the spectator may ask what has made the pupil of the man portrayed dilate. Perhaps it has spotted an opportunity or threat. The result may be anger, horror, or euphoria. The mouth open in aggression or scream of fear is simultaneously gagged with an irregular solid put in it by the artist. We do not know whether it is an external object or a deformed body part, which may be indicated by its colour identical to that of the whole face. The businessman with the face of Janus is cracking a problem or is gagged by someone, something, or the situation. Something 'sticks in his throat' or someone is 'ramming something down his throat', something that he is forced to accept.

The elegant grey and regular geometry of the buildings in the background stand in contrast with the madness and hysteria of a businesswoman with her caricatured body shape filled with loud coloured areas in the artistic vision by Peter Saul. In *Businesswoman* (1987–1990), we see a satirically represented and extremely expressive character whose absurd figure along with her office interior design (a red carpet, rich armchair) stand in contrast to the formal, grey, geometric background formed by typical office buildings in the business district of a big city – and make the impression of incongruence and inconsistency with that environment. The painting contains elements of caricature, humour, irony and shows the manner of nonchalance, or even airiness, in addressing serious matters, characteristic of the artist. After all, the works of Saul criticize such institutions as the government, big business or . . . the feminist movement[53] (www.georgeadamsgallery.com/artists/peter-saul, accessed: 3.08.23). Certain oppositions are evident. The luxurious, colourful world created by the character portrayed for herself contrasts to the organized, grey external world. Internal chaos – personified by the *businesswoman* by the absurd, non-anatomical position of her legs, indicating her lack of control, even self-control, her one-eyed face with animal features, the nose resembling a pig's snout – contrasts here to the tidy external world. The colourfulness stands in contrast to the grey environment and office buildings situated in perspective. The accessories shown in the painting, such as telephone handsets, live their own lives and are out of control or treated carelessly, which is indicated by their arrangement. The big mouth and pig's snout in place of the nose evoke associations with self-indulgence, but the eye, although the only one, remains attentive and still. It warns us to be careful and not disregard the woman.

The one-eyed individual in the picture may be associated with the Cyclops, who was a character of enormous strength but also easy to outplay due to his limited field of vision. This may be the case of the businesswoman in the picture, who, despite the satirical and caricatured features she has been given by the artist, is depicted in a richly equipped corner office on a high level – undeniable attributes of power and influence.

This version of art is described as antagonistic, aesthetically drawing from cubism with extremely immature, grotesque figures. The artist himself defines the subject matter as nothing so complicated as the brutal underbelly of American excess – it is like turning over a rock in the woods and seeing what crawls out (from the article 'Peter Saul Doesn't Want Any Advice', Max Lakin, 13 July 2021, www.nytimes.com/2021/07/13/t-magazine/peter-saul-art.html, accessed: 3.08.23).

The area of organization and management seems to be a 'producer' of contrasts, divisions, and boundaries. Some people are seated in huge armchairs, with postures expressing nonchalance and confidence; others are clients of employment agencies, charitable organizations, or struggle to survive taking any job, also that situated between a rubbish tip and the district of wealth, the world of finance visible in the background. The artist's sensitivity casts the world of organizations and its people in the role of the producer of inequality and divisions.

4.2.8 The organization as a system

Organizations are systems. In representing the organization as an abstraction, artists illustrate connections between its components, environment, and results of actions taken. The system corresponds to a structural rather than a process-oriented perception of the organization, although it also assumes that the configurations of its constituent parts are subject to temporal variation.

The organization can be metaphorically imagined as a set of geometric forms on a grey background, neutral in its emotional value. The space is dominated by white rectangular forms, complemented on the right of the composition by smaller ones in yellow, bright green, and red. The dominant structure of vertical and horizontal lines is split by separate diagonals – some seem to be parts of more specific forms that might resemble schematically outlined faces; on the left of the composition; others seem to constitute – in the work's central part – a system of connections suspended in space, something like levers or pistons actuating each other. The black irregular area right in the centre of the composition introduces an element of tender line in this otherwise rigid composition. Such an image of the organization is proposed in a work by Arshile Gorky (1904–1948), an Armenian immigrant to the United States. His *Organization*,[54] dated 1933–1936,[55] is a coherent composition where forms completely fill the plane. Something is contained in something else or overlaps something else. This is a system of co-existing harmonious forms. Their similarity suggests a certain schematic indicating a reciprocal effect of individual components. The composition is dynamic and suggests the organization's coming to existence. The joints of lines resemble bearings with a mechanism operating inside, where the circular forms are flywheels.

Who knows, maybe analysis of artworks could have led at an earlier time to the opinion proposed by Walter Buckley in 1967, arguing that morphogenesis 'refers to those processes which tend to elaborate or change a system's given form, structure or state' (Buckley, 1967, p. 58). It seems that the hypothesis about the morphogenesis of social systems, including organizations, could have been hidden in artworks of the interwar period.

An abstractionist representation of the organization is also seen in *Organization No. 21* by John Sennhauser (1907–1978) from 1942.[56]

This vision of the organization is much less expressive, it can be said: minimalist in its form and message, elegant. The work's plane is distinctly divided into quarters – like a chart, a geometric coordinate system. Square forms in various shades of grey, smaller, bigger, contained in one another, sometimes disregard the division of space and cross its boundaries – quite like illustrations of the dynamics of phenomena that can vary from increasing to decreasing values, from negative to positive ones. There are verticals, horizontals, and the line arrangement harmonizes with stable and regular forms contained in the composition. The plane is divided partly symmetrically (by the vertical line) but there is also considerable free space, and forms are loosely arranged. Possible artefacts, schematically outlined, are organized around some central idea, symbolized by a thick, unfinished axis. That axis of symmetry may indicate the pillar of the organization – unilaterally suspended, anchored from the top and tending to the counterbalance marked with a white line in the bottom of the composition.[57]

Both abstractionist representations of the organization provoke a thought about its mechanical nature. The system in this understanding is a set of structural components, reciprocally oriented on a plane, which means that they can operate in a specific configuration and interconnection.

Another vision of the system is proposed in *Business as Usual* from 1992 by Jason Rhoades (1965–2006). This collage consists of multiple photographs and pictures. It features photographs of people in suits, of political assemblies in combination with greeting cards containing various slogans or posters with clearly propaganda messages. This artwork can be interpreted as an illustration of a process, continual cycle of actions that are constant despite changing times and circumstances. There is a veiled accusing statement that disapproves of reaping profit on any opportunity, especially on war. This work by Rhoades is a special depiction of a phenomenon and idea by negation, meaning that we receive a message about something that actually is missing in the picture – something that is not shown or rather there is the absence of something illustrated. In this interpretation, the collage shows the absence of morality. We see a system of interrelations and connections between various agents. The consequences of their actions are suffered by others – marginalized people with no influence on their lives and situations. This message encourages resistance to pressure. The work is the antithesis of propaganda, and its hidden but legible narrative reveals the dirty side of business.

Societies and organizations are autopoietic systems[58] that produce their own components, define their boundaries and structure, are self-producing, and each of their operations depends on previous operations and information they gathered (Luhmann, 1997, p. 65). They are capable of replication, self-organization, even self-production, can resolve some conflicts to provoke others, which is perfectly illustrated in the described artwork.

4.2.9   *Existential framework and windows of opportunity*

The environment in representations of business may have a varying character but its characteristic feature is the potential for setting frameworks for human, and especially business activity. Indeed, each course in management aims to teach students basic analytical tools, such as SWOT, where strengths and weaknesses are internal to the organization while opportunities and threats come from the environment, or basic classifications considering micro, macro or competitive environment, to name a few examples. Various forms of framing the depicted situation or person are also characteristic of paintings where they become literal windows through which to look at reality or metaphorical frameworks that determine or simply limit one's living space.

The London artist Christopher Richard Wynne Nevinson, A.R.A. (1889–1946)[59] in his 1916 work *From an Office Window* depicts in a quite claustrophobic, closed composition a system of power lines and geometric forms. In his work, the non-depicted is also important. The plane is completely filled with an industrial landscape, a geometric layout where nature is absolutely absent. Its grey and blue colour scheme, cool colour shades, simply industrial in their cold character, fill the office window. The window is a symbol of sight and perspective. It can be a 'windows on the world', which created by corporations and the industrial revolution while geometrically treated forms suggest *novus ordo* of a formatted, structured world. The dominant position of the observer of that world that we see through a window, having a view from above, may indicate that this world is owned by the observers from the office, is created by them. And perhaps those who have this view are only silent recipients of changes made by someone else which they cannot influence and may only observe a limited, rather uninspiring fragment of reality, a fragment that defines the space of their daily existence.

The windows open to space in a melancholy painting by Hopper *Office in Small City*, although free from panes, seem to be a limitation. The bright colour scheme of this painting and the space filled with natural light, reflected by bright walls, does not create, unlike the landscape in *From the Office Window*, any depressing or dark aura. Nevertheless, the work is received as an illustration of a boundary between two worlds: that in the office on the top floor of a building and that situated far on the horizon, and looked for by the seated character. There is a limitation, a form of alienation, a difference between that 'what is' and that 'what could be'. Can we see here a 'window of opened-up opportunities' or rather a structure resembling a metaphorical ivory tower where the melancholy, alienated character has closed himself or has been closed?

A quite different framing of space in representations of business are financial institutions that set a framework for our economic existence. They are depicted in this function in the 1939 painting *The Cathedrals of Wall Street* by Florine Stettheimer.

We see an assembly of public personae surrounded by symbols and figures of finance, dominated by the building of the New York Stock Exchange. Politicians are treated in this composition equally with leading representatives of banking institutions, such as J.P. Morgan or D. Rockefeller. The gathering is diversified in their social background, roles, and ethnicity.

The centre of the composition is occupied by representatives of high society; observers are situated on the right side, and the antithesis of wealth or a symbol of conscience of the wealthy is situated in a corner: this is a stand of the Salvation Army. The work is the apotheosis of corporatocracy, and the existential framework created by cooperating private businesses, financial entities, and politicians is depicted as huge, framing edifices of financial institutions. The work shows celebration. Is it a celebration of the capitalist system, market institutions, or economic freedom?

The central section of the work is dominated by the classical-style edifice of the New York Stock Exchange, and framing is formed by the monumental structures of bank buildings. Far deep in perspective, we can see the Statue of

Liberty as a symbol of values. Its situation in the painting, in perspective, but in the far distance, may inspire questions. Is it a symbol of values that recede? How much have we departed from them? Are they our axiological roots that we originate from as businesspeople? Are they our early origins, something to be remembered, or a goal to be achieved?

The artist was familiar with high society and celebrity, as a member of the wealthy New York establishment. A contemporary of Andy Warhol, she portrayed American pop-culture, although in a relatively conservative manner, regarding her technique and means of expression. Critics argue that she depicted New York as it was, openly manifesting her affection or even admiration for the city. *The Cathedrals of New York* is a series of four works illustrating secular religions of Manhattan, begun in 1929 at the outbreak of the Great Depression. The paintings represent the foundations of New York life: money, show business, museums, and galleries showing socio-political life and the commercial aspect of life – that is, Fifth Avenue. *The Cathedrals of Wall Street* is a picture of big money and connections between the worlds of politics and business; characteristically, main figures in the entire series are not those who are celebrated but those who celebrate and admire secular cathedrals and temples of secular worship. When looking at the compositions, their colour schemes, the thought comes to our minds of their similarity to the poster form. The artwork is composed like the cover of a colour magazine, with the proper theme of representation situated in the composition's centre, a crowd of figures observing those situated below, and a relatively large space left at the top (Gopnik, A., How Florine Stettheimer Captured the Luxury and Ecstasy of New York, 21 February 2022 (www.newyorker. com/magazine/2022/02/28/florine-stettheimer-artist-book-review-barbara-bloemink, access: 3.08.23). The marginal situation of representatives of the Salvation Army in the left bottom corner is open to interpretation: a warning against temptations offered by the financialized (in today's terminology) world; a reminder of the poor and needy, or perhaps arousing conscience and appealing for charity?

Notes

1. See Organizational Advances (philamuseum.org).
2. See Jolan Gross Bettelheim | Employment Office | The Metropolitan Museum of Art (metmuseum.org).
3. See www.metmuseum.org/art/collection/search/283353.
4. In the set of photographs of business figures, a series of photographs of a single individual frequently appeared, either in very similar or different positions, although usually in similar contexts or situations.
5. See Walker Evans | [68 Portraits of M. J. Rathbone of Jersey Standard Oil, for Fortune Business Executive Profile] | The Metropolitan Museum of Art (metmuseum.org).

6. There is also an interesting 2014 drawing with the same title where the figure of a businessman is depicted as a compact composition of geometric forms, with dominant, randomly distributed detached eyes and an ear, while the whole gives the impression of forms packed in a schematic outline of a suit. The works can be seen on George Condo | The Businessman | Drawings Online | The Morgan Library & Museum, accessed: 28.08.2023).

7. We distinguished in the coding phase office wear from conventional wear. In the first case, as the term indicates, only those works were coded that represented figures in evidently office interiors. In the other case, we interpreted the category of conventional wear more extensively as typical of a specific situation, not necessarily limited to office interiors but also including space outside, for example, when figures are portrayed during travel or a casual meeting in the street.

8. Certain code categories were insufficiently represented and were not included in the tables due to their low occurrence frequency, but still they are worth mentioning, as they may be indicative of certain isolated fragments of marginal narratives.

9. See Cameron & Quinn, 2015.

10. See Arieli et al., 2020.

11. See Walker Evans | [19 Portraits of Carleton of 3M, for Fortune Business Executive Profile] | The Metropolitan Museum of Art (metmuseum.org).

12. The complete code structure is presented in an appendix.

13. We adopt a classical understanding of this concept as an antonym of 'slave' in a general sense and a word referring to an individual who enjoys full freedom in ethical choices, makes them independently, and is free from any constraint. This type of freedom in life, resulting from a sufficiently high financial position giving independence, from exercising capital owner's rights and allocating capital, is characteristic of people running small and medium-sized businesses and forming the middle class.

14. Spinoza wrote, for example, this sentence: 'Homo liber de nulla re minus, quam de morte cogitat, et ejus sapientia non mortis, sed vitae meditatio est', meaning 'a free man thinks of death least of all things; and his wisdom is a meditation not of death but of life' (Huenemann, 1997, p. 115).

15. The man portrayed by Degas is actually in his thirties.

16. Portraits à la Bourse is held by Musée d'Orsay. In its oil version, the picture clearly shows architectural structures in the form of impressive classical-style columns – an element so frequently used to create certain symbolism of corporate buildings and thus appearing in paintings in a less or more metaphorical manner. An example is seen in *The Cathedrals of Wall Street* by Florine Stettheimer.

17. See 'London Stock Exchange, a typical young businessman', Emil Otto Hoppé, 1937 | Tate.

18. See Christopher Richard Wynne Nevinson, A.R.A. (1889–1946) (christies.com).

19. See Walker Evans | [330 Views and Studies of Brown Brothers Harriman & Company Bankers, Their Offices, and Employees at Work, and Related

Views of Partners' Residences, Commissioned by Doubleday & Company for 'Partners in Banking', Published 1968] | The Metropolitan Museum of Art (metmuseum.org).

20. See Edward Hopper | Office in a Small City | The Metropolitan Museum of Art (metmuseum.org).
21. Compare Walker Evans | [148 Portraits and Studies of Bankers at Work Including Joseph Barr, Probably Commissioned by Fortune Magazine] | The Metropolitan Museum of Art (metmuseum.org).
22. See 'Charity Organization Society', Henry Tonks | Tate.
23. See 2011_CSK_03693_0022_000(maria_lassnig_geschaeftspartner085020). jpg (203×150) (christies.com).
24. See Untitled (Office Workers) (nga.gov).
25. André Arbus (1903–1969) was a furniture and interior designer and a sculptor. He was director of the École nationale supérieure des Arts Décoratifs.
26. See Jason Rhoades (1965–2006) (christies.com).
27. See Florine Stettheimer | The Cathedrals of Wall Street | The Metropolitan Museum of Art (metmuseum.org).
28. See 'Henry Crispe of the Custom House', Thomas Frye, 1746 | Tate.
29. See Traveling Business Man, Rhineland (Reisender Kaufmann, Rheinland) (Getty Museum).
30. See http://collections.walkerart.org/item/object/191.
31. See New York Office, 1962, by Edward Hopper.
32. See https://medium.com/dipchain/jacob-lawrence-the-businessmen-bca 8c22e7f5a.
33. See www.nga.gov/collection/art-object-page.84864.html.
34. See www.metmuseum.org/art/collection/search/485934.
35. See www.tate.org.uk/art/artworks/wright-thomas-staniforth-of-darnall-co-york-t00794.
36. The depicted man's involvement in slave trade does not seem to affect the way he is portrayed. In the time of the creation of this work, this type of business did not provoke general ethical reflection. The question then is to what extent those facts known about the biography of the man portrayed may affect perception and reception of the work. Can the brown colouring of the background and business wear be associated with the symbolism of making 'dirty' money or 'dirtying one's hand'?
37. We analyse a pastel (study) from the Met for a painting held at Musee d'Orsay. See www.metmuseum.org/art/collection/search/436154.
38. See www.christies.com/en/lot/lot-6034443.
39. See www.metmuseum.org/art/collection/search/259997.
40. Also today, organizations are not free from stereotypes. Is not their persistent existence demonstrated by such phenomena as the 'glass ceiling', discrimination evident, for example, in the gender pay gap or mobbing?
41. Justice has to be done to the author, who depicts young businessmen in an equally caricatured way that is not free from obscenity. The painting Young Business can be viewed here: www.artsy.net/partner/blondeau-and-cie/works?artist_ids%5B0%5D=peter-saul, accessed: 16.09.2023. In addition, this is strikingly illustrated in *Homme d'affaires chinois fondant*

sur Wall Street (see *https://blogs.mediapart.fr/luc-rigal/blog/101112/la-grande-moquerie-picturale-de-peter-saul* 28.08.2023).

42. We conducted a pilot survey consisting of open interviews with five representatives of the upper managerial class and entrepreneurs (CEOs, investors and firm owners) – initially, to build a classification of codes that might be used for the purposes of analysis. We finally decided not to use that method of acquiring knowledge due to considerable temporal differences between the works analysed and thus potentially inadequate assessments of the modern business community as made by today's representatives.
43. Henry Tonks was a British medical professional, surgeon, and later draughtsman and painter, known for his sceptical attitude towards progressive ideas. After the outbreak of the First World War, he returned to practising medicine, and he gained his painter's fame through a series of pastels showing patients – soldiers – before and after plastic surgery. He had a 'surgical' eye for drawing (www.npg.org.uk/whatson/display/2014/henry-tonks-studies-of-the-artist, access: 3.08.23). See www.tate.org.uk/art/artworks/tonks-charity-organization-society-t11004.
44. Benjamin Truman (1700–1780) was a wealthy businessman under whose management the *Truman Brewery* in London developed into one of the largest, if not the largest, business of this type in the then world.
45. See 'Sir Benjamin Truman', Thomas Gainsborough, c.1770–4 | Tate.
46. Historical details about the Black Eagle Brewery and its development under the management of Sir Benjamin can be found here: www.british-history.ac.uk/survey-london/vol27/pp116-122, accessed: 3.08.23.
47. See https://pl.pinterest.com/pin/18155204724801857/ and www.getty.edu/art/collection/object/107R7Y#full-artwork-details.
48. See Lucian Freud (1922–2011) (christies.com).
49. Working-class affinity (recent social advancement); see the figures from J. Stainbeck (2022).
50. The dictionary edited by W. Doroszewski contains references to various publications that give definitions of individual concepts. This also applies to the word 'phenomenon'. Doroszewski refers to 15 various sources in which the word is defined.
51. It is worth mentioning that there is a sketch for this painting with another character's arrangement and clothing, Study for Office at Night 1940, where the receptionist wears a dress with long sleeves, and while looking for something in documents, she turns her head to the figure at the desk, also turning his body towards her – the characters seem to have a conversation based on information that the man sitting at the desk is finding in documents that he is holding in hand and studying (https://whitney.org/collection/works/6299, accessed: 3.08.23).
52. George Condo (born 1957) described his painting as 'artificial realism', and his characters, originating from the absurdity of everyday life, are multi-dimensional. The artist represents in a single portrait multiple personality of one character, creating a kind of psychological cubism (George Condo interview in Financial Times by Julie Belcove, www.ft.com/content/038b3f86-a8d8-11e2-bcfb-00144feabdc0, accessed: 3.08.23).

53. An interesting illustration of satire in perceiving business is given in another work by Saul titled Young Business, 1969, that was not included in the original set of works subject to analysis, as it appeared at auction in the Blondeau & Cie gallery that was not entered in the list of our sources. That work, containing a considerable portion of obscenity, is an iconic example of lampooning business. Interesting conclusions can also be drawn from a work by the same artist titled *Businessmen 7*. Both artworks can be viewed here: www.artsy.net/partner/blondeau-and-cie/works?artist_ids%5B0%5D=peter-saul, accessed: 16.09.2023.
54. See www.nga.gov/collection/art-object-page.56937.html#inscription.
55. The mysterious art of Arshile Gorky, William Feaver, 6.02.2010; www.theguardian.com/artanddesign/2010/feb/06/arshile-gorky-painting-william-feaver, accessed: 3.08.23.
56. See John Sennhauser | Organization No. 21 | The Metropolitan Museum of Art (metmuseum.org).
57. The artist has painted more organizations that were not included in the basic set of works subject to analysis due to their location outside major auction houses and museums, but we must mention, for example, Organization 17 that is like a kite in the wind, demolishing symmetrical verticals and horizontals, where the line arrangement harmonizes with stable, regular forms and structures resembling ladders.
58. 'Autopoiesis' is a term introduced by two Chilean researchers and referring to biology or, more precisely, to the chemistry of living cells. The authors observed the capability of the cell to regulate its own activity using complex processes resembling in part communication (Maturana & Varela, 1980). Luhmann applied this concept in analysis of social systems and organizations. He also attaches great importance to communication in social systems, emphasizing in the case of organizations the role of decision as a form of communication (Luhmann, 2000, p. 185).
59. The artist was clearly influenced by the futurists and chose quite versatile subject matters for his paintings; however, his main inspiration became the dark themes of war during the First World War. We see in his work a cubist manner (with whom he had exhibited in 1915). (https://gerrishfineart.com/artist/c-r-w-nevinson/, accessed: 3.08.23).

Conclusion
Looking at ourselves in the pupil

During our dialogue about interpretations of works relating to the area of organizations and management and emotions that may be provoked by those aesthetic communications, we initially did not consider the existing body of particular knowledge of the works that gave us inspiration. In omitting the formal description of a work and its context, both historical and social and special, relating to the individual style and manner of the artist, we aimed at preventing the influence of external suggestions in the course of analysis and identifying the original connotations aroused by perception of the work. We consider those connotations to be a reflection of the latent knowledge referred to in the methodological note.

If we finally decided to include in our analysis elements of formal knowledge of the artists, contexts, and figures represented in the works, this was aimed at illustrating the possibility of the co-existence of multiple narratives. The question of whether artwork as an aesthetic communication can transmit narratives and provide a basis for an alternative tale, constructed separately from the formal assumptions and facts underlying its origin, should be answered cautiously. It seems that there is a certain layer of universal content that becomes evident regardless of the historical period and particular social context in which the work was created. Valuable conclusions may be drawn from a comparison of two works created in various times and contexts, but they still show certain universal phenomena, although in strikingly different ways.

A historical example, distant in time, is given by the painting that depicts tax gatherers and criticizes parsimony and avarice, draws attention to the threat of corruption in the sphere of municipal officials.[1]

Here is a room occupied by tax collectors – with rich wainscoting and a lot of documents and sealed records untidily spread on the cabinet in the background. In the foreground, we see two figures with a quite repulsive appearance, sitting at a table lined with green broadcloth. The character on the left is writing something with a quill in a leather-bound book. The character on the right, sitting close, is looking with an unpleasant grimace at the spectator, slightly leaning over the table on which a handful of coins is put. Presumably,

DOI: 10.4324/9781003497103-6

his role is to count and perhaps give correct amounts to be recorded by the other official. His grimace expresses ruthlessness. They have old faces with saggy skin, sharp noses, bony hands with distinct lines of veins. The attire of both officials is bizarre; although their clothes seem to be rich, with fur trims around necks and cuffs, their head coverings are quite curious, making the figures look somewhat grotesque and perhaps even ridiculous. The painting *Two Tax-Gatherers* originates from the workshop of Marinus van Reymerswaele (1533–1545) about 1540; it depicts two ugly figures wearing clothes that are bizarre even from the perspective of the historical period in which the painting was created. The characters are most probably municipal officials, and the documents relate to municipal funds. The painting criticizes corruption and avarice, considering that tax collectors received commissions conditional on tax amounts they managed to collect (www.nationalgallery.org.uk/paintings/workshop-of-marinus-van-reymerswale-two-tax-gatherers, accessed: 3.08.23). The painting shows the division of roles in the absence of hierarchical diversification. The figures wear similar clothes. They differ in emotional intensity – one of them, perhaps from the first line of contact with taxpayers, is highly emotional in his facial expression, while the other, attending to the record, is dispassionate. The work can be seen as a depiction of a system that in its properties represented by the two figures has remained unchanged – a system that can be described in terms of insensitivity, ruthlessness, and institutional corruption, considering the previously indicated way of remunerating officials. The painting shows certain dynamics of public institutions that are responsible for managing municipal funds, which should be perceived as a valuable and commendable role, on the one hand, but are susceptible to misconduct and, for sure, commonly disliked, on the other hand. This resentment is clearly felt in the work's atmosphere.

An illustration showing a specific system, but referring to phenomena observed globally (which is not surprising in a work created recently), is given in the collage by Jason Rhoades (1965–2006) with a meaningful title *Business as Usual*. It represents systemic, and repeated in the historical cycle, interrelations between the spheres of politics, propaganda, secret business, and armed conflicts, which despite promoted anti-war slogans invariably create a favourable environment for continuing practices aimed at maximizing profit. When looking at combined, in a quite paradoxical way, photographs of gentlemen in dark suits – figures evoking associations with dealings discussed at the table and resulting in backstreet transactions completed at a warehouse ramp or car – pictures of political manifestations, demonstrations, or posters promoting anti-war slogans in the manner of greeting cards – we get the impression that the collage tells about recurring history with the repetition of systemic phenomena related to reaping benefits from armed conflicts, to pronouncing at manifestations empty slogans that are never realized, with building veiled, unclear structures of power and influence where the sphere of ideals, or simply ideology, politics, is intertwined with the sphere of business.

Public finance, managing municipal funds, and the taxation system are also *business as usual*, and there is a perpetual discussion on excessive fiscal burdens carried by enterprises and by the population and on mismanagement of funds by those who hold public offices (see: https://www.un.org/development/desa/en/wp-content/uploads/2020/07/RECOVER_BETTER_0722-1.pdf).

The question arises, 'To what extent can artwork as an aesthetic communication transmit universal narratives, and to what extent can it provide a basis for an alternative tale, constructed separately from the formal assumptions and facts underlying its origin?' In other words, can communication live its own life? There are multiple reasons for an affirmative answer; the simplest example is given by the origin and life of a rumour, which is also a communication, but while continually repeated, it is reconstructed so that its message with a meaning different from the original one lives its own life. However, it is an ephemeral life. The power of rumour is exhausted time, and the message vanishes. On the other hand, an artistic communication is recorded by the artist, so abstracting the message from its author becomes more difficult and problematic. However, adopting the concept of 'open work', we see that not everything is determined by the artist, and the spectators or audience have much to say. They finally decide what to accept as a message and what to reject, putting in question the role of artists as sole managers of their works. Artworks are also managed by art galleries with their marketing actions, critics, or specialist and popular magazines that shape the preferences of art purchasers. A message that is abstracted from the artist and lives its own life may be contained in paintings by an unknown artist who suddenly becomes famous – galleries, art dealers, and collectors begin to compete for the works. What makes it happen? Perhaps, the media set a fashion for the works. If so, the message began to live only in the rhythm of fashion.

Thus, it seems that the potential of an aesthetic communication for living its own life and being interpreted in a way completely different from the artist's purpose is not an inherent feature of artworks but rather a question of certain intentionality on the part of the spectator. The works that we discussed are historically diverse and created in various periods, and consequently the subjects that they represent and the way of representation may be a resultant not only of an individual artist's manner but also of dominant period schools, styles, and fashions in the areas of painting and drawing, and of a specific social context. Still, in addition to their contextual layer, they do carry a message that is universal to a considerable extent.

However, the indicated contextual aspect of artworks and the evolution of means used to represent reality related, for example, to styles in painting lead to reflection on possible trends or stereotypes that are observable in aesthetic messages and correspond to trends of simply fashions in management and organizational thought. In our opinion, this correspondence exists. It is evident in reception of the founders of the classical management theory, their fascination with functionality, simplicity, and later ergonomics. Reflections of this approach can be found in works of interior designers, architects, in the 'industrial style' or 'industrial design', and its presence is still observed in projects of various types and on various scales. Interaction between management and art is evident in the works of Walter Gropius and the design school he founded, known as Bauhaus. Gropius argued that Bauhaus should provide design for mass production, design that should be simple, rational and available to everyone. He believed that design of all types should be inspired by clearly stated problems and their solutions should in turn result from the rule: form follows function (Volkes & Harrison, 2020).

For example, abstractionist works may be associated with relatively recent aspects of management theory, such as virtual organization or a systemic approach to the organization, and may be well suited for describing those aspects due to the concise, simplified or even minimalist form of expression characteristic of abstractionism. Minimalism can especially be associated with the departure from formal hierarchies, and thus making organizational structures flat or liberating the organization from its anchors in the form of traditional buildings, offices, properties and relocating it to the virtual, digital sphere where it can freely reconfigure itself, like geometric forms floating in space, as shown in the 1942 watercolour by John Sennhauser (1907–1978) titled *Organization No. 17*.[2] However, it can be noted that the word 'abstraction' (from *abstrahere* – detach from, drag away, remove) means that we have to do with a kind of modelling, distinguishing certain aspects of reality or 'detaching' from concrete events, people, groups and situations with the aim of representing them in a more general form that can be referred to multiple specific objects. In this sense, abstraction can be interpreted with reference to both advanced management methods and such topics as leadership or conflict.

Traditional, perhaps even classical, topics in management theory, such as bureaucracy or an expanded organizational hierarchy, are represented by works following the aesthetic of figurative art, with clear contour or expressive colour areas, which is well illustrated in *Untitled (Office Workers)* by Schultheis or Saul's *Business Woman*. An interesting experiment could be tried including a detailed analysis of the evolution path of management theory and modern painting styles, with addressing the question whether a correlation exists between the manner of perceiving reality in aesthetic messages and the manner of assimilating reality and the business environment as proposed in various approaches to management.

When looking at aesthetic representations of the business world and its figures, we can easily be tempted to seek rules that would indicate the existence of certain aesthetic characteristics attributable to archetypal business figures, such as the player or official, or canonical business phenomena, such as the contrastive or systemic nature of the world of organizations. Attempts at defining dominant aesthetics of the organization may not lead to generalizations, and constitute only a kind of idiosyncrasy resulting from specific characteristics of material under study, just like case studies in management are focused on specific details. However, those attempts indicate the fact that a certain set of means of artistic expression can potentially be more or less capable of representing the world of organizational phenomena. Table C.1 contains a summary of artistic elements describing selected code categories.

Table C.1 Categories of representing business and means of artistic expression

	Composition	Colour	Chiaroscuro	Expression
Player[3]	Closed, static	Dominant cool colours regardless of the colour scheme width	soft modelling with light	Realistic representation with attributes characteristic of the profession
Official[4]	Open, static, coherent, multi-plane, filled with similar figures; a character focused on work in the centre	Monochrome or a narrow colour scheme with dominant cool colours, a classical painting perspective, contrasts black/white, slants	n/a	Realistic representation with attributes characteristic of the profession
Contrasts[5]	Closed, symmetric	Wide colour scheme, saturated colours in the foreground, value contrasts	Artificial light, sharp form modelling	Illusory representation, strong colour areas, attributes of profession and symbolism
System[6]	Closed, symmetric, verticals, horizontals, slants, clear divisions of the plane	Dominant cool colours, contrasts white and black, attenuated by grey accents	n/a	Prevailing play with line, but also strong colour accents, saturated

Source: Own elaboration

The figure of 'player', frequently situated in a closed and static composition with dominant cool colours, is represented realistically with soft light modelling. This brings to mind the composure of such figures, the nuanced nature of the situation, and the fact that players create their own worlds in which they remain the central and unique element.

Dominant cool colours and a static composition are also characteristic of works depicting the figure of 'official', although open compositions occur more frequently in this set, sometimes with strong contrasts (e.g. white-black). The world of officials is repetitive and may be reproduced by adding more identical elements, going beyond the framework that confines an individual, standardized person similar to others.

Organizational contrasts are illustrated using means of aesthetic illusion, hard light modelling, strong colour areas, and a wide scheme of saturated colours. Finally, 'system' is frequently represented using a play of lines, symmetries, and clear divisions of the painting plane, with a dominant cool colour scheme, sometimes reduced to emotionless grey tones.

Another question that inevitably arises when we look at the way the artists perceive the world of organizations is about the art of representation as contrasted to committed art. A comparison of the two works described above, strikingly different and created in different periods, confirms the formation of an evaluating and socially committed discourse about business and business-related questions.

An attempt to overcome the rigidity of research methods sanctioned by tradition, in both teaching and publications, and set out on an intellectual journey along new paths, must inevitably lead to reflection on limitations resulting from such an approach.

In view of the fact that part of works in our research material are portraits of specific individuals with specific faces and mimics, we can consider to what extent the message carried by those works is representative for specific ways of depicting business and to what extent it generates observations with an anthropological nature. In other words, an interesting path of future analysis could be indicated by answering the following question: To what extent the represented figures are typical for a widely understood business profession, and to what extent they are only selected from many examples of figures from their historical period.

The question of representativeness of figures for a specific profession certainly does not exist in the case of photographs taken as part of the series Fortune Business Executive Profile, as these works exemplify icons of management and business, and thus model figures, respected for their achievements. However, considering the fact that the photographs were taken by a single artist, the question may be asked: to what extent that representativeness can be affected by some bias in the way of portraying, a tendency resulting from the photographer's artistic manner. An interesting line of future research can be seen in a comparison of a greater number of photographic portraits done by various fine-art photographers; this would allow to reveal specific features of representations of business figures while also considering the effect of the specific nature of the means of expression used.

Most works included in the research material reflect mainly the American point of view. It seems that its domination is rather natural because management as a discipline has its origins in the United States and, as regards Europe, in France or Great Britain. Research material was sampled from online-available collections held by leading American and European museums and auction houses; however, an expanded set of sources, including other museum institutions, also from outside Europe, and art galleries as a source of potential aesthetic messages, could provide additional research material and promising new directions in analysis, which certainly is worth considering. However, the domination of the American point of view in the sample we analysed is partly counterbalanced by its eclectic character. The analysis included both historical and contemporary works, created using various techniques and representing various styles; thus, it was made using a kind of triangulation adequate to the characteristics of the research material.

There is some risk that by carrying out our analysis using inductive reasoning and open coding, we may project onto the reader our own idiosyncrasies – which seems to some extent acceptable in qualitative research. Indeed, a researcher operating in the interpretative and constructivist paradigm does not avoid emotional involvement in the analysed material. Additionally, the purpose of artworks is to generate experiences of an aesthetic nature – that is, qualified as those we like and those we dislike, those pleasant and those irritating to see.

Appreciating the existing considerable achievements of organizational aesthetics and drawing inspiration from the results of our experiment on aesthetic material, we see a number of research opportunities that are worth considering. We focused our study on visual material: paintings, graphics, and photographs. Since a platform for interpreting the organization and the way it achieves its goals can be provided not only by artefacts in the form of paintings and graphics, it is worth considering what vision of the world of organizations is carried by messages originating from other arts, for example architecture. There are interesting studies that focus on the symbolism contained in architectural works, which carries a message of values important for an organization and is sometimes used as a tool of power and domination (Barnes & Newton, 2019; Kerr & Robinson, 2016); nevertheless, it would be interesting to carry out an analysis of interior architecture and find an answer to the question of how the design of commercial or work space influences the process of achieving organizational goals, especially building relations, maximizing sales, teamwork, or creativity. These questions are inevitable and related to the concepts of organizational identity and organizational culture, since aesthetic messages constitute an integral part of both. Indeed, the visual identity of an organization consists of messages based on language, typography, line, colour, and shape. Logo design and typography become a form of organizational tale and thus can provide excellent material for the analysis of the aesthetic characteristics of various industries.

This book identifies a direction in organizational experiences in which art performs the role of a signpost, enabling observers to gain a new insight into reality in which they do not participate and customers and employees to develop emotional relationships and a feeling of identification (or lack of identification) with the organization. Assuming that art, with the wealth of its artefacts and forms of expression, constitutes a kind of membrane that allows to selectively structure the relations between the organization and its environment, the importance of art for a qualitative improvement of management and leadership capabilities becomes evident. Workshops on creative expression, painting, or drawing can complement hard managerial skills, shedding new light on certain nuances – for example, where the line should be stronger and where it should be subtle; where to apply a more distinct colour area, or a glaze to soften tones and colours of the underlying paint layer; and how to distribute light and dark. Those decisions are dictated not only by the technique learned but also by sensitivity, which in management is equally important as skillful operation in the sphere of numbers, processes, and technology. Sensitivity indicates how to use tools.

Finally, a promising field of research on organizational aesthetics is defined by the interrelation between the world of art and that of business as an active investor and agent, being not only an object of artistic representations but also a subject that actively shapes the art market. Big financial corporations, private investors, professional company managers amass art collections, either for purely prestige-building, hedonistic, or investment purposes. A reasonable question arises: To what extent are the aesthetic preferences of a period shaped by business and organizations that considerably contribute to institutionalization and commercialization of artistic activity? Thus, to what extent artworks created at a moment or in a period of time reflect the tastes of particular groups – investors – and to what extent they are unrestricted expressions of artistic visions? The influence of big corporations on culture in today's world cannot be reasonably denied, and this is why, considering the quality of common aesthetic experience, key importance must be attached to those factors that create cultural capital – that is, sensitivity and tradition – without them, any attempts at building up collections must turn into mere snobbish cultivation of bad taste instead of being admirable acts of philanthropy.

Notes

1. See www.nationalgalleryimages.co.uk/asset/1955/.
2. See www.mutualart.com/Artwork/Organization-No–17/742D0C08CAF
   923C2.

3. For example, in Degas E., Portraits at Stock exchange, Derby, J.W. of, Thomas Staniforth of Darnall, Co. York and Dix, O., The Businessman Max Roesberg, Dresden.
4. For example, Schultheiss, C., Untitled/Office Workers and Pieter de Josselin de Jong, In the office.
5. For example, Condo G. The Business Man and Saul P., Business Woman.
6. For example, Gorky A., Organization and Sennhauser J., Organization no 21.

Appendix 1
Visual data list

A list of analysed visual data – paintings (accessed 28.08.23)

Arbus A., 1935, Design for an Office, www.metmuseum.org/art/collection/search/343357

Bettelheim J. G., 1943, The Employment Office, www.metmuseum.org/art/collection/search/374843

Condo, G., 2007, The Businessman, www.christies.com/en/lot/lot-6128037

de Josselin de Jong P., In the Office, www.christies.com/en/lot/lot-6034443

Degas E., Portraits at Stock exchange, www.metmuseum.org/art/collection/search/436154

Dix O., 1922, The Businessman Max Roesberg, www.metmuseum.org/art/collection/search/485934

Freud L., 1948, A Walk to the Office, www.christies.com/en/lot/lot-5698846

Frye, T., 1746, Henry Crispe of the Custom House, 'Henry Crispe of the Custom House', Thomas Frye, 1746 | Tate

Gainsborough, T, c, 1770, Sir Benjamin Truman, www.tate.org.uk/art/artworks/gainsborough-sir-benjamin-truman-t02261

Gorky A., Organization, 1933–1936, www.nga.gov/collection/art-object-page.56937.html#inscription

Hopper E., 1953, Office in a Small City, www.metmuseum.org/art/collection/search/488730

Hopper E., 1940, Office at Night, http://collections.walkerart.org/item/object/191

Hopper E., 1962, New York Office, www.edwardhopper.net/new-york-office.jsp#prettyPhoto[image2]/0/

Lassnig M., 1919, Geschaeftspartner (Business Partners) www.christies.com/img/LotImages/2011/CSK/2011_CSK_03693_0022_000 (maria_lassnig_geschaeftspartner085020).jpg?height=150

Lawrence J., 1947, The Businessmen, https://medium.com/dipchain/jacob-lawrence-the-businessmen-bca8c22e7f5a

Nevinson, Ch. R. W., A.R.A. 1918, From an Office window, www.christies.com/en/lot/lot-6088224

Potter, A., 1933–1936, Organizational Advances, https://philamuseum.org/collection/object/341487

Reymerswale M. van, ca. 1540, Two Tax-Gatherers, www.nationalgalleryimages.co.uk/asset/1955/

Rhoades J., 1992, Business as Usual, www.christies.com/en/lot/lot-4955620

Saul P., 1987–1990, Business Woman, www.christies.com/en/lot/lot-5437418

Schultheiss, C., ca. 1950, Untitled/Office Workers, www.nga.gov/collection/art-object-page.146895.html

Sennhauser J., 1942, Organization No. 21, John Sennhauser | Organization No. 21 | The Metropolitan Museum of Art (metmuseum.org)

Sennhauser, J., 1942, Organization No. 17, www.mutualart.com/Artwork/Organization-No – 17/742D0C08CAF923C2

Stettheimer, F. 1939, The Cathedrals of Wall Street, www.metmuseum.org/art/collection/search/488733

Tonks, H., Charity Organization Society, www.tate.org.uk/art/artworks/tonks-charity-organization-society-t11004

Wright of Derby, J., 1769, Thomas Staniforth of Darnall, Co. York, www.tate.org.uk/art/artworks/wright-thomas-staniforth-of-darnall-co-york-t00794

A list of analysed visual data – photographs (accessed 28.08.23)

Evans W., 19 Portraits of Carleton of 3M, for Fortune Business Executive Profile, www.metmuseum.org/art/collection/search/283346

Evans W., 25 Portraits of Clifford F. Hood of U.S. Steel, for Fortune Business Executive Profile, www.metmuseum.org/art/collection/search/283354

Evans, W., 1941, Three Businessmen, National Bank Building Entrance, Florida, www.getty.edu/art/collection/object/104A6S

Evans W., Two Businessmen: for the series 'Dress', https://pl.pinterest.com/pin/18155204724801857/

Evans, W., 1941 Business Man, Bridgeport, Connecticut, www.getty.edu/art/collection/object/107R7Y#full-artwork-details

Evans, W., 49 Portraits of McCloy of the Chase, for Fortune Business Executive Profile, www.metmuseum.org/art/collection/search/283355

Evans, W., 4 Portraits of McCollum of Continental Oil, for Fortune Business Executive Profile, www.metmuseum.org/art/collection/search/283352

Evans, W., 23 Portraits of Russell of Southern Pacific, for Fortune Business Executive Profile southern1, www.metmuseum.org/art/collection/search/283348

Evans, W., 14 Portraits of Craig of AT&T, for Fortune Business Executive Profile, www.metmuseum.org/art/collection/search/283344

Evans, W., 148 Portraits and Studies of Bankers at Work Including Joseph Barr, www.metmuseum.org/art/collection/search/279152

Evans, W. 68 Portraits of M. J. Rathbone of Jersey Standard Oil, for Fortune Business Executive Profile, www.metmuseum.org/art/collection/search/283366

Evans, W., Two Businessmen in Hats Talking on Street, Florida, www.met museum.org/art/collection/search/259997

Evans, W., Portrait of F.W. Ecker of Metropolitan Life, www.pinterest.com/ pin/walker-evans-f-w-ecker-of-metropolitan-life-for-fortune-business-executive-profile-1953–483292603736568054/

Evans, W., Portrait Kaiser-Fraser's, 38 Views of Kaiser-Fraser's Automobile Plant and Portraits of Executives, Ypsilanti, Michigan, Commissioned by Fortune Magazine for 'Adventures of Henry and Joe in Autoland', www. metmuseum.org/art/collection/search/279261

Evans, W., 330 Views and Studies of Brown Brothers Harriman & Company Bankers, Their Offices, and Employees at Work, and Related Views of Partners' Residences, Commissioned by Doubleday & Company for 'Partners in Banking', www.metmuseum.org/art/collection/search/27914

Evans W., 30 Portraits of Ganger of Lorillard, for Fortune Business Executive Profile, www.metmuseum.org/art/collection/search/283353

Evans W., 4 Portraits of F. W. Ecker of Metropolitan Life, for Fortune Business Executive Profile, www.metmuseum.org/art/collection/search/283363

Evans, W., 27 Portraits of Vickers of Sperry, for Fortune Business Executive Profile, www.metmuseum.org/art/collection/search/283356

Frank, R., Man in Office – Butte, Montana, National Gallery of Art, www.nga. gov/collection/art-object-page.84864.html

Hoppe, E.O., London Stock Exchange, a typical young businessman, www. tate.org.uk/art/artworks/hoppe-london-stock-exchange-a-typical-young-businessman-p13382

Sander A., 1930, Travelling Business man, www.getty.edu/art/collection/objec t/1041A7

Sander A., 1927, Young Businessman, www.moma.org/collection/works/193986

Sander A., 1930–1935, Business Manager of a Theatre (Kaufmännischer Di-rektor eines Theaters), www.getty.edu/art/collection/object/1041JF

Appendix 2
Code books

Table A1 Code structure, phase 1 (predefined codes complemented inductively)

Code tree

Communication objective
  Providing knowledge
  Encouraging reflection
  Arousing emotion
  Exemplification
  Persuasion
Authority
  Competence-based
    Making decision
    Instructing, disciplining
    Supervising
    Clarifying, explaining
  Asset-based
    Possessing information
    Attributes of power
  Based on attitude towards others
    Proud, dominating posture
    Calm, composure, confidence
    Proud/brave sight
Subject of communication
  Active
  Passive
Figure characteristics in communication
Physical
  Repulsive appearance
    Caricatured
    Rigidity
    Ugliness
  Individualization
    Unconventional clothes
    Typological differentiation
  Dominating the scene
    Attractiveness

(*Continued*)

Table A1 (Continued)

Code tree

      Plumpness
      Ease
      Nonchalance
    Figure impersonality
      Anonymity
      Standardization
    Conventionalism
      Elegance
      Office wear
      Conventional wear
    Negative emotional states
      Melancholy
      Sadness
      Frustration
      Depression, fatigue
  Personality
    Working and professional
    Persistence, resolution
    Multitasking
    Risk-taking
    Strict meticulousness
    Mindfulness
    Concentration
  Situational
    Cunning
    Humility
    Provocative
    Calm, composure
  Relational
    Duplicity, hypocrisy
    Confidence
    Suspiciousness, cautiousness
    Detachment
    Unlikeability
    Communicativeness
    Likeability
    Secrecy
    Curiosity
Values
  Focusing values
    Professional orientation
    Future orientation
    Competitive struggle
    Aggression
  Competing values
    Efficiency
    Achievements
    Growth

(*Continued*)

Table A1 (Continued)

Code tree

Profits
Results
Continual improvement
Adaptivity
Innovation
Creativity
Entrepreneurship
Stability
Formalization
Discipline
Security
Centralization
Control
Interpersonal relationships
Teamwork
Cooperation
Care for others
   Helping others
     Institutional
     Interactive (individual)
Trust
Organizational vs individual values
Creativity
Money
Success
Life comfort
Expression of individuality
Respect for others
Prestige
Customer service
Product quality
Integrity
Honesty
Innovation
Stability of the organization and budget
Value for community
Utilitarianism
Tolerance of diversity
Employee well-being
Company reputation
Leadership in an industry
Sense transfer methods
By exegesis
By correlations
By context
Subsumption/exclusion
By opposition
Communication direction

(*Continued*)

Table A1 (Continued)

Code tree
Unfavourable
Neutral
Favourable
Topic of communication
Group
Event
Organization
Institution
Person
Process
Habitat, environment

Source: Authors own elaboration

Table A2 Code structure, phase 2 (open coding, emergent themes)

Code tree
Attributes of management
Telephone
Walking staff
Quill, fountain pen
Papers
Folders
Record
Relationships
Domination
Indifference
Lack of interest
Alienation
Lack of bonds
Cooperation
Stereotypes and conventions
Stereotypical roles and behaviours
Clothing convention
Breaking the clothing convention
Approach to tasks
Solving a problem
Waiting for decisions
Chaos
Hierarchical work organization and bureaucracy
Consultations
Perception
Non-oriented sight
Oriented sight

(*Continued*)

Table A2 (Continued)

Code tree

    Concentration
Time
  Windows on the world
  Passing time
  Longing for the next step
  Memory of the past
Environment
  Situational framework
    Depressing environment
    Confinement
  Existential framework
  Reaction to the environment
    Fight for individual positions
    Being an integral part of the environment
    Surrender
    Distance
    Approach to risk
      Conservatism
      Balance
      Risk-taking
Space
  Economical space organization
    Minimalism
    Figures packed together
  Formatting
  Spatial hierarchy
    Organizational foundation
    Segmentation
    Dominant structure
  Organizational depth
Community
  Team
  Influential actors
    Propaganda
  Community of losers
    Losers, passive
    Losers, active
  Community of the endangered
  Community of the wealthy
Business figures
  Official
    Performing the role
    Indifference
    Meticulousness
    Standardization
  Player
    Frustration, depression
    Reflection

(Continued)

Table A2 (Continued)

Code tree

Reserve
Adaptation to circumstances
 Diversity
Eccentricity
Astuteness
Aggression
Duplicity
Confidence
Doggedness
Haughtiness
Position of power
Cunning
Determination
Avarice
 Thoughtlessness – fixation
Homo liber
Plumpness
Physical attractiveness
Homo liber/calm
Cheerful disposition
Elegance
Ease
 Nonchalance
Hedonism
Illustration of a phenomenon
Corporatocracy
Secrecy
 Indefinite character
Contrasts and duplicity
Corporate hierarchy
Prestige
Decline
System
Marginalization
 Alienation

Source: Authors own elaboration

Bibliography

Achterkamp, M. C., & Vos, J. F. J. (2008). Investigating the use of the stakeholder notion in project management literature, a meta-analysis. *International Journal of Project Management, 26*(7), 749–757.

Arieli, S., Sagiv, L., & Roccass, S. (2020). Values at work: The impact of personal values in organisations. *Applied Psychology, 69*(2), 230–275.

Armstrong, D., Gosling, A., Weinman, J., & Martaeu, T. (1997). The place of inter-rater reliability in qualitative research: An empirical study. *Sociology, 31*, 597–607.

Babbage, C. (1835). *On the economy of machinery and manufactures.* Charles Knight.

Baer, M. D., van der Werff, L., Colquitt, J. A., Rodell, J. B., Zipay, K. P., & Buckley, F. (2018). Trusting the "look and feel": Situational normality, situational aesthetics, and the perceived trustworthiness of organizations. *Academy of Management Journal, 61*(5), 1718–1740. https://doi.org/10.5465/amj.2016.0248

Barnard, C. (1983). *The functions of the executive.* Harvard University Press, Cambridge.

Barnes, V., & Newton, L. (2019). Symbolism in bank marketing and architecture: The headquarters of national provincial bank of England. *Management & Organizational History, 14*(3), 213–244.

Barrett, F. J. (1998). Coda-creativity and improvisation in jazz and organizations: implications for organizational learning. *Organization Science, 9*(5), 605–621.

Baudrillard, J. (1970). *Société de consommation. Ses mythes, ses structures.* Editions Denoël.

Beckman, S., Scott, S., & Wymore, L. (2018). Collaborative innovation: Exploring the intersections among theater, art and business in the classroom. *Journal of Open Innovation: Technology, Market, and Complexity.* https://doi.org/10.3390/joitmc4040052

Bellah, R. N. (1985). *Habits of the heart: Individualism and commitment in American life.* University of California Press.

Berelson, B. (1952). *Content analysis in communication research.* Free Press.

Berle, A., & Means, G. (1932). *The modern corporation and private property.* Commerce Clearing House.

Beyes, T. (2017). Colour and organization studies. *Organization Studies, 38*(10), 1467–1482. https://doi.org/10.1177/0170840616663240

Biehl-Missal, B., & Springborg, C. (2015). Dance, organization, and leadership. *Organizational Aesthetics, 5*(1), 1–10.

Bigler, R. S., & Liben, L. S. (2006). A developmental intergroup theory of social stereotypes and prejudice. In R. V. Kail (Ed.), *Advances in child development and behavior* (Vol. 34, pp. 39–89). Elsevier.

Black, I. S. (1996). Symbolic capital: The London and Westminster Bank headquarters, 1836–38. *Landscape Research, 21*(1).

Bourdieu, P., red. (1993). La misere du monde. Paris: Editions du Seuil.

Brady, F. N. (1986). Aesthetic components of management ethics. *Academy of Management Review, 11*(2), 337–344.

Buckley, W. (1967). *Sociology and Modern Systems Theory.* Englewood Cliffs: Prentice-Hall.

Burnham, J. (1941). *The managerial revolution.* Putnam&Co., Ltd.

Cameron, K. S., & Quinn, R. E. (2015). *Kultura organizacyjna – diagnoza i zmiana. Model wartości konkurujących, wyd. II.* Wolters Kluwer.

Campbell, J. L., Quincy, C., Osserman, J., & Pedersen, O. K. (2013). Coding in-depth semistructured interviews: Problems of unitization and intercoder reliability and agreement. *Sociological Methods & Research, 42*(3). https://doi.org/10.1177/0049124113500475

Carr, A., Hancock, Ph eds. (2003). *Arts and Aesthetics at Work.* Palgrave Macmillan. Hampshire and New York.

Clark, T., Mangham, I. (2004). From dramaturgy to theatre as technology: the case of corporate theatre. *Journal of Management Studies, 41*(1), 37–59.

Cole, A. L., & Knowles, G. L. (2008). Arts-informed research. In W. J. G. Knowles & A. L. Cole (Eds.), *Handbook of the arts in qualitative research. Perspectives, methodologies, examples, and issues* (pp. 55–70). Sage.

Conway, H., Roenisch, R. (2005). *Understanding Architecture: An Introduction to Architecture and Architectural History.* London-New York: Psychology Press.

Doroszewski, W. (Red.). (1963–1969). *Słownik języka polskiego.* Państwowe Wydawnictwo Naukowe (t. 5–11). Retrieved August 28, 2023, from https://doroszewski.pwn.pl/haslo/zjawisko/

Doroszewski, W., (ed.) (1996–1997). "zjawisko" [entry in the dictionary]. in: Słownik języka polskiego. Warszawa: Państwowe Wydawnictwo Naukowe, https://doroszewski.pwn.pl/haslo/zjawisko/ (accessed 28.08.2023).

Dovey, K. (1999). *Framing Places. Mediating Power in Built Form.* London: Routledge.

Easy Rider. (1969). Dir. D. Hopper. Pando Co and Raybert Productions.

Eco, U. (1994). Dzieło otwarte. In *Forma i nieokreśloność w poetykach.*

Elias, N. (2007). *The court society.* UCD Press.

Freeman, R. E. (1984). *Strategic management: A stakeholder approach.* Pitman Publishing Inc.

Freeman, R. E., & Reed, D. L. (1983). Stockholders and stakeholders: A new perspective on corporate governance. *California Management Review, 25*(3), 88–102.

Gelman, S. A., & Roberts, S. O. (2017). How language shapes the cultural inheritance of categories. *Proceedings of the National Academy of Sciences of the United States of America, 114*(30), 7900–7907.

Giddens, A. (1984). *The constitution of society: Outline of the theory of structuration: Elements of the theory of structuration*. University of California Press.

Glaser, B., & Strauss, A. (1967). *The discovery of grounded theory*. Aldine de Gruyter.

Godin, B. (2001). Defining R&D: Is research always systematic? *Project on the History and Sociology of S&T Statistics*, *7*, 2–18.

Goffman, E. (1981). *Człowiek w teatrze życia codziennego*. PIW.

Govers, R., & Go, F. M. (2005). Projected destination image online. Website content analysis of pictures and texts. *Information Technology & Tourism*, *7*(2), 73–89. https://doi.org/10.3727/1098305054517327

Hancock, P. (2005). Uncovering the semiotic in organizational aesthetics. *Organization*, *12*(1), 29–50. https://doi.org/10.1177/1350508405048575

Heath, J. (2009). The uses and abuses of agency theory. *Business Ethics Quarterly*, *19*(4), 497–528.

Heilbroner, R. L. (1993). *21st Century Capitalism*. New York: Norton.

Homayoun, S., & Henriksen, D. (2018). Creativity in business education: A review of creative self-belief theories and arts-based methods. *Journal of Open Innovation: Technology, Market, and Complexity*, *4*(4), 55. https://doi.org/10.3390/joitmc4040055

Huenemann, C. (1997). Spinoza's free man. *Journal of Neoplatonic Studies*, *6*(1), 105–133.

Hyman, M., & Renn, J. (2012). *Towards an Epistemic Web*. http://doi.org/10.2139/ssrn.2104137

Kalinka, W. (1885). *Jenerał Dezydery Chłapowski*. Poznań.

Kerr, R., & Robinson, S. (2016). Architecture, symbolic capital and elite mobilizations: The case of the royal bank of Scotland corporate campus. *Organization*, *23*(5), 699–721.

Kolbe, R. H., & Burnett, M. S. (1991). Content-analysis research: An examination of applications with directives for improving research reliability and objectivity. *Journal of Consumer Research*, *18*, 243–250.

Komander, V., & Konig, A. (2022). Organizations on stage: Organizational research and the performing arts. *Management Review Quarterly*, *74*(4), 1–50. https://doi.org/10.1007/s11301-022-00301-9

Kramer, M. W., Crespy, D. A. (2011). Communicating collaborative leadership. *Leadership Quarterly*, *22*, 1024–1037.

Krippendorff, K. (2004). *Content analysis: An introduction to its methodology* (2nd ed.). Sage.

Krokos, J. (1998). Metody fenomenologiczne i ich aktualność: Zarys problemu. *Studia Philosophiae Christianae*, *34*(2), 103–111.

Kuhn T.S., Obiektywność, sądy wartościujące i wybór teorii, in: Kuhn T.S., Dwa bieguny. *Tradycja i nowatorstwo w badaniach naukowych*, PIW, Warszawa 1985.

Kumaniecki, K. (Ed.). (1976). *Słownik łacińsko – polski*. PWN.

Lavoi, D. (1994). Odkrywanie i postrzeganie szansy gospodarczej: Kultura a Kirznerowski model przedsiębiorczości. In B. Berger (Ed.), *Kultura przedsiębiorczości*. Oficyna Literatów "Rój", Warszawa.

Leavy, P. (2015). *Method meets art. Arts-based research practice*. The Guilford Press.

Leavy, P. (2018). Introduction to arts-based research. In P. Leavy (Ed.), *Handbook of arts-based research* (pp. 3–21). The Guilford Press.

LeBaron, C., Jarzabkowski, P., Pratt, M., & Fetzer, G. (2018). An introduction to video methods in organizational research. *Organizational Research Methods, 21*(2), 239–260.

Lekka-Kowalik, A. (2010). Nauka wolna od wartości – groźna utopia współczesnej kultury. In E. Jarmoch, Jarmoch E., Świderski A. W., Trzpil I. A., (Eds.), *Bezpieczeństwo człowieka a wartości: zbiór prac. Aspekty filozoficzne i edukacyjne* (T. 1). Wydawnictwo Akademii Podlaskiej.

Liedtka, J. M. (1989). Value congruence: The interplay of individual and organizational value systems. *Journal of Business Ethics, 8*(10), 805–815. https://doi.org/10.1007/BF00383780

Lombard, M., Snyder-Duch, J., & Bracken, C. C. (2002). Content analysis in mass communication: Assessment and reporting of intercoder reliability. *Human Communication Research, 28*(4), 587–604. https://doi.org/10.1111/j.1468-2958.2002.tb00826.x

Luhmann, N. (1997). *Die Gesellschaft der Gesellschaft*. Suhrkamp Verlag.

Luhmann, N. (2000). *Organisation und Entscheidung*. Westdeutscher Verlag.

Lüscher, L. S., & Lewis, M. W. (2008). Organizational change and managerial sensemaking: Working through paradox. *Academy of Management Journal, 51*(2), 221–240.

Maher, M. A. (2000). Diagnosing and changing organizational culture: Based on the competing values framework. *Journal of Organizational Change Management, 13*(3), 300–303.

Mallac, G. D. (1971). The poetics of the open form: Umberto eco's notion of "Opera Aperta". *Books Abroad, University of Oklahoma, 45*(1).

Mangham, I. (1990). *Managing as a performing art*. https://doi.org/10.1111/j.1467-8551.1990.tb00166

Mannay, D. (2010). Making the familiar strange: Can visual research methods render the familiar setting more perceptible?. *Qualitative Research, 10*(1), 1–37.

Martikainen, J. (2018). The promise of visual approaches in organizational and management research. In W. Thomas, A. Hujala, S. Laulainen & R. McMurray (Eds.), *The management of wicked problems in health and social care* (pp. 235–249). Routledge.

Martikainen, J. (2019). Visual arts-based research methods in social science research. *PEOPLE: International Journal of Social Sciences, 5*(2), 323–345.

Maturana, H., & Varela, F. (1980). *Autopoiesis and cognition: The realization of the living*. Reidel.

May, R. (1994). *The courage to create*. W.W. Norton.

Merton, R. K. (1982). Struktura biurokratyczna i osobowość. In Wiatr, J.J. (Ed.), *Teoria socjologiczna i struktura społeczna* (pp. 255–266). Warszawa: PWN.

Nonaka, I., & Takeuchi, H. (2000). *Kreowanie wiedzy w organizacji*. Poltex.

Nowotny, H., Scott, P., & Gibbons, M. (2003). Mode 2 revisited: The new production of knowledge. *Minerva, 41*, 179–194.

Pauwels, L. (2010). Visual sociology reframed: An analytical synthesis and discussion of visual methods in social and cultural research. *Sociological Methods & Research, 38*(4), 545–581.

Popping, R. (1992). In search of one set of categories. *Quality and Quantity, 26*, 147–155.

Preston, K. B., & Jean-Louis, K. (2020). A community service organization focused on the arts to develop empathy in pharmacy students. *American Journal of Pharmaceutical Education, 84*(4).

Rain Man. (1988). Dir. B. Levinson. United Artists.

Ramachandran, R. (2019). Theories of stakeholder management. *SSRN Electronic Journal.* https://doi.org/10.2139/ssrn.3535087

Rehr, D. E., & Zaniello, J. (2017). Diversity and inclusion. Core values among associations. Vetted Solutions.

Renn, J. (2022). *The evolution of knowledge. Rethinking science for the anthropocene.* Princeton University Press.

Reymont, W. S. (2020). *Ziemia obiecana.* Bellona, Warszawa.

Richardson, B. J. (2019). Green illusions: Governing CSR Aesthetics. *Windsor Yearbook of Access to Justice, 36*, 3–35. https://doi.org/10.22329/wyaj.v36i0.6065

Ritzer, G. (1999). *Enchanting a Disenchanted World: Revolutionizing the Means of Consumption.* Thousand Oaks, CA: Pine Forge Press.

Ritzer, G. (2010). *Enchanting a Disenchanted World: Continuity and Change in the Cathedrals of Consumption.* L.A. SAGE.

Riza, S. D., Heller, D. (2015). Follow your heart or your head? A longitudinal study of the facilitating role of calling and ability in the pursuit of a challenging career. *J Appl Psychol, 100*(3), 695–712.

Rubin, H. J., & Rubin, I. S. (2005). *Qualitative interviewing: The art of hearing data* (2nd ed.). Sage.

Schechner, R. (2003). *Performance theory.* Routledge.

Schumpeter, J. (1960). *Teoria rozwoju gospodarczego.* PWE.

Shortt, H. L., & Warren, S. K. (2017). Grounded visual pattern analysis: Photographs in organizational field studies. *Organizational Research Methods, 22*(2), 539–563.

Snyder M., Tanke E. D., Berscheid E. (1977). Social perception and interpersonalbehavior: On the self-fulfilling nature of social stereotypes. *Journal of Personalityand Social Psychology, 35*(9), https://doi.org/10.1037/0022-3514.35.9.656

Sombart, W. (2010). *Żydzi i życie gospodarcze.* IFiS PAN.

Stainbeck, J. (2022). *Grona gniewu.* Prószyński i Spółka.

Sternberg, E. (1997). The iconography of the tourism experience. *Annals of Tourism Research, 24*(4), 951–969.

Strati, A. (2009). Do you do beautiful things? Aesthetics and art in qualitative methods of organization studies. In D. Buchanan & A. Bryman (Eds.), *The Sage handbook of organizational research methods.* Sage.

Sun, Y., & Latora, V. (2020). The evolution of knowledge within and across fields in modern physics. *Scientific Reports, 10*, 12097. https://doi.org/10.1038/s41598-020-68774-w

Sztompka, P. (1991). *Society in action. The theory of social becoming*. The University of Chicago Press.

Thelma&Louise. (1991). Dir. R. Scott. Metro Goldwyn-Mayer.

Thomas, R., Sargent, L. D., & Hardy, C. (2011). Managing organizational change: Negotiating meaning and power-resistance relations. *Organization Science*, *22*(1), 22–41.

Tsay, C-J. (2013). Sight over sound in the judgment of music performance. *Proceedings of the National Academy of Sciences*, *110*(36), 14580–14585.

Volkes, J., & Harrison, S. (2020). *Bauhaus Zeitgeist. The Architecture of Walter Gropius. Bauhaus 1919 to 1923: Radical innovations in design education*. Bauhaus Archive Berlin, Museum of Design.

Voss, G. B., Cable, D. M., Voss, Z. G. (2000). Linking organizational values to relationships with external constituents: a study of nonprofit professional theatres. *Organ Sci*, *11*(3), 330–347.

Warren, C. A. B., Karner, T. X. (2010). *Discovering Qualitative Methods. Field Research, Interviews, and Analysis*. Oxford University Press.

Weber, M. (1999). *Obiektywność poznania w naukach społecznych"* tłum (M. Skwieciński, Ed.). Problemy socjologii wiedzy, PWN.

Weber, R. P. (1990). *Basic content analysis* (2nd ed.). Sage.

Weick, K. E. (1992). Agenda setting in organizational behavior. *Journal of Managerial Inquiery*, *1*(3), 171–182.

Weick, K. E. (1998). Introductory essay: Improvisation as a mindset for organizational analysis. *Organization Science*, *9*(5), 543–555.

Whitehead, A. N. (1938). *The Aim of Philosophy. Lecture Nine in Modes of Thought*. New York: Macmillan.

Witkin, R. W. (2009). *The aesthetic imperative of a rational-technical machinery: A study in organizational control through the design of artifacts*. www.researchgate.net/publication/38105677_The_Aesthetic_Imperative_of_a_Rational-Technical_Machinery_A_Study_in_Organizational_Control_Through_the_Design_of_Artifacts

Wölfflin, H. (2006). Podstawowe pojęcia historii sztuki. *Problem rozwoju stylu w sztuce nowożytnej*. Gdańsk: słowo/obraz.

Wölfflin, H. (2009). *Principles of art history*. Göteborgs universitet.

Wölfflin, H. (2015). *Principles of art history: The problem of the development of style in early modern art: One hundredth anniversary edition*. Getty Publications.

Index

Note: Page numbers in *italic* indicate a figure or chart and page numbers in **bold** indicate a table on the corresponding page.

relaxed confidence 44–47, **45**
research, management 21–23; aesthetics of the organization 23–25; architecture of metaphors and associations 32–33; content in visual objects 25–32
research programmes 14; debate 16–18, *17*; dialogue 15–16; elementary research situation 14–15; narratives 18–19
Russell of Southern Pacific (Evans) 30

secrecy 55, **56**, 89–92, **114**, **118**
sense transfer methods 26, 42, 44, 51, **115**; by context 26, 41, **115**; by correlations 26, 44, **115**; by exegesis 26, 41, **115**; by opposition 26, 41, **115**; subsumption/exclusion 26, 42, **115**
similarities, neutral 36–44, *36–37*, *39*, *41*, *43*
space 3, 25–33, 78–82, 86, 93–96; of emergent values 51–71; formatting 62, **117**; minimalism 62, 104, **117**; organizational depth 62, **117**; of secrecy and contrasts 89–92; spatial hierarchy 62–63, **117**
stereotypes 79–81
success 48–51, **50**
system 9–11, 30, 55–57, 78, 92–94, 102–103

temples 2, 24, 96
Thomas Staniforth of Darnall, Co. York (Wright of Derby) 75–76, 89

time: longing for the next step 68, *69*, **70**, **117**; memory of the past 68, *69*, **70**, **117**; windows on the world *59*, 68, **70**, 95, **117**
Travelling Business Man (Sander) 30
travelling entrepreneur 87–88
Two Businessmen: for the Series 'Dress' (Evans) 30, 88
Two Businessmen in Hats Talking on Street, Florida (Evans) 30, 40, 79
Two Tax-Gatherers (Reymerswale) 102

Untitled (Office Workers) (Schultheiss) 47, 78, 80

values: in business 48–51, **50**; competing values 27, 48, **50**, **114**; emergent 51–72, **52**, *55*, **56**, *58–59*, **61**, *64–65*, **66–67**, *68–69*, **70**, *71*; focusing values **50**, **114**; organizational values 27, 44
Vickers of Sperry, for Fortune Business Executive Profile (Evans) 30, 35n9
visual experiences 21–23; aesthetics of the organization 23–25; architecture of metaphors and associations 32–33; content in visual objects 25–32

Walk to the Office, A (Freud) 88
windows of opportunity 94–96

For Product Safety Concerns and Information please contact our EU
representative GPSR@taylorandfrancis.com
Taylor & Francis Verlag GmbH, Kaufingerstraße 24, 80331 München, Germany

www.ingramcontent.com/pod-product-compliance
Ingram Content Group UK Ltd.
Pitfield, Milton Keynes, MK11 3LW, UK
UKHW020928280425
457818UK00025B/51